RAILTOWN ALMANAC

Railtown
Almanac
A Spokane Poetry Anthology

Edited and introduced
by Jeffrey G. Dodd and Thom Caraway

Sage Hill
Press
Spokane, WA

Railtown Almanac: A Spokane Poetry Anthology
Copyright © 2014 Sage Hill Press
ISBN: 978-0-9890359-4-1
All Rights Reserved
Printed in the United States

For permissions and ordering information contact:

Sage Hill Press / 1848 W. Bridge Avenue
Spokane, Wash. / 99201

or visit www.sagehillpoetry.com

Book design by Jeffrey G. Dodd

Cover design by Matt Comi
Back cover poem and illustration by Vachel Lindsay

Contents

Preface
Jeffrey G. Dodd and Thom Caraway

This book is our effort to build a testament to the rich poetic terrain of the Inland Northwest. There are better poets than us: in Spokane, in our offices, probably in our houses. But we think we're pretty good advocates. Spokane has always had great poets, whether they teach at a university or a high school, wait tables or make coffee, or none of the above. There are as many ways to be a poet as there are poets.

Lucky for us, Spokane has something going on, something unusual and special. Terrific writing communities have existed in Spokane for years: EWU's Inland Northwest Center for Writers, the Spokane Poetry Slam, the Beacon Hill Reading Series at Spokane Community College, and dozens of other school-based, coffee shop-based, and independent groups. There is a genuine spirit here, and it can be seen in the groups that come to the many events: Broken Mic, Get Lit!, Ink Art Space, the Wordwright Workshops, SpoPo, various university reading series, Spokane Poetry Slams at Boots Bakery and the Bartlett. And more keep popping up. Not only are there enough writers to support all these events, but there's an audience as well.

Along with these events, we have the Spokane Arts Fund, a bold public/private organization that helps support the arts across our city. The Arts Fund supports juried shows, First Friday, mural projects, film projects, and countless other endeavors.

In the last decade, artists around Spokane seem to have emerged from a long winter, poked their heads up, and found that they could change the city they lived in: underpasses, bridges, and a long-time downtown eyesore have been rejuvenated by new murals; sculptures have popped up in new parks and along urban trails; letters to Spokane light up the sides of buildings; newspapers and weeklies run innovative creative pieces, and compilations like *Spokane Shorties* and *Lilac City Fairy Tales* suddenly appear in the hands of a diverse and engaged reading public. And this is in addition to the individual achievements of our writers: Jess Walter, Shawn Vestal, Sharma Shields, Shann Ray, Kris Dinnison, Julie Riddle; Laura Read, Ellen Welcker, Tod Marshall, Laurie Lamon, Cathy Bobb, D.S. Butterworth, Nance Van Winckel; Spokane Grand Champion Chris Cook, and our other representatives at the Individual World

Poetry Slam: Emily Gwinn, Kurt Olson, and Katie Schmarr. Awards, bestsellers, new books, national recognition, and a genuine spirit of comradery and inclusiveness.

We've tried to represent a broad cross-section of the poetry being written in and about our city. And we're grateful to present high school and college students, established writers of all ages and career stages, and even a few who probably don't self-identify as poets. There are poets who've lived here their whole lives, and some who tried to record the mark left on them as they passed through our city.

We know we've missed great writers. And some of our best slam poets were victims of limited space in these pages. We look forward to the chance to make amends for these oversights and limitations in future volumes.

We'd like to extend special thanks to the estates of Vachel Lindsay, the original Spokane poet, and Tom I. Davis, a great local advocate lost too soon. We also extend many thanks to Hailee Meyers, who has handled contracts, proofs, and myriad other small details that we wouldn't have otherwise been able to handle. We are especially grateful to Melba Slater, who came forward with a generous micro-loan to help finance the printing of the anthology. This is the kind of community art activism we hope will proliferate around Spokane and allow under-the-radar projects to flourish.

Ours is a city full of great writers who aren't just content to sit at home and write. They want to build the community. And, in a city like Spokane, they can. And they do.

This book is dedicated to all of those writers.

Jeffrey G. Dodd and Thom Caraway
October 2014

11 Notes Before Midnight

Anastasia Aguon

11:00 I promise not to hurt you

11:01 so that's what blood looks like

11:03 for courage to stay right where you are, imagine your suicide on repeat.

11:07 I fall asleep next to a man who holds me like his dead best friend. He will have a daughter someday—I dream about a six year old with her favorite black beret sleeping in Mom's bed so the darkness won't eat her up.

11:11 police officers pick up a body
    two belt marks are found on your upper thigh and one hole under the
        breast,
    barely any blood to clean up picks up off the sheets
    private parts have always been a good place to hide secrets and other
        bodies.
    your small family will be forced to speak to each other in the dark,

    you want them to look up
    come what may, some things will always be there,
    like the stars

11:20 I wake up to your breath on my shoulder. You are still alive. I don't know why this surprises me. The blood in the sink is embarrassing. I flush the toilet. Slip back into bed.

this is not an accident.

11:44 that blood is beautiful so put it right here in the microphone.
it is the only place where you can toss suicide notes and the darkness eats them.

11:50 no one teaches you depression is a medical condition or a
       marriage proposal.

It does not define you.
all this—is yours.

They will call your death an accident.

11:57 I want them to know my love is not an accident.

12:00 I promise you he can't hurt me. Only the darkness can do that and it
asks "do you want me to take you home?"

No.

Carrying a Canvas, Midnight: Downtown Spokane

Zan Agzigian

for Derek Eliasen

The moon hung flawlessly crowned,
a three-quarter Chihully: A flacon,
spilling Ode to Midnight down
upon Sprague Avenue past red fox letters
towering the sky: A friend stopped,
switched hands, as we held his oversized
canvas on the street. The wind

indiscreet, made his painterly
forms seem like glass in
the moonlight, gave the illusion the red-
hot reds were sliding to the pavement:
a fiery Fall leaf fluttering
to the grave vase-earth.

Canvas: Moon: Vessel of white,
we held tight, switching hands again,
resting the tips of the painting on our shoes
(my toes curled) giving amber and yellow
new meaning in the streets.
Art Angels: The Moon, Gabriel,
you, Me: Yod en Yod hauling celestial spirals,
traffic light humming, a-hounding our pace.
We are cyclical, giving ourselves up
after all this work: martyred
by the vast blackboard universe above.

Walking on alone, around a corner after: blue neon
Swims on the window of a Ford. Below
The Spokane River opens its mouth in swirls
To drink whatever illumination life
Has to give, waiting for the hidden warrior to shoot
The stars for one more cup of crystal night.

I Spent My Summer Nights on the Patio of the Old Empyrean [154 S. Madison]

Mark L. Anderson

because we were young

because being young is stupid

because we do not get a million nights

because age sticks its fingers into the spine

because our story didn't take long to tell

because the years ahead were quicksand
already sucking at our feet

because the train endlessly leaving town
is the spirit animal of every twenty something
year old in this city of bricked up dreams

because when are we going to be famous?

because love is hard like the falling apart
concrete walls of an ancient train trestle

because we fancied ourselves the kings of the place

because we wanted to save rock and roll
we wanted to save poetry

because everyone laughed at us

because some of the people in this story
have already died

because innocence is a lightning bug
fading away in the smog heavy sky

because we were not original, yet

because I didn't realize then that this
would be a time worth telling

because youth is nearly the same thing
as being restless

because we spoke before we listened
correction: we shouted instead of listening

because we could feel the quicksand
at our feet

because childhood ends mid-sentence

because the black-wire tables cast in starlight
spoke to us of freedom

because desperation was our language
ancient as DNA

> In this place
> we bricked together our stories
> never once realizing
> what they would come to mean.

Blood Moon Birthday

Liv Larson Andrews

Four times 'round the sun
we sing for you with candles.
Your teacher tells of the rainbow bridge, the starry gate,
the storied entrance you still make
into each day.

I recall darkness at your entry, too,
like the passage made
by slaves under moonlight.
Blood on the doorposts hallowing their way
stepping in safety through parted waters.

You came through a watery passage
to a wilderness path.
Four years along and wilder still
each morning a new telling,
the ruddied moon bearing witness.

Breach

Derek Annis

My mother stood on the side
of the highway with a box
full of teeth in her left hand, the keys
to the red convertible,
against which she was leaning,
in her right. She asked me
which I would like to have,
but being so small, and having eaten
so much sand, I was ill
prepared to answer.
She held out the box full of teeth
and told me to watch
them for her until
she could return. Then she turned
from me, got into the red convertible,
turned the key, laid rubber
on the road and revved off
the edge of the earth.
I have been waiting here
by the side of the highway,
and I have tried to care
for the teeth, but now
and again the crows come
steal one from me
while I sleep.

Celebration in the Room of Broken Light

Derek Annis

The silver-dollar-sized spider living in the corner
of my ceiling—hollowed out
silk-bound insects snagged
in its symmetrical web—is God, so I slide
a chair across the room, step up
onto it, smash Him with the heel of my palm,
smear His guts on the wall, and wipe away
the web with little effort. In this instant
all the world's priests shrivel and drop
from the pulpit like rotten plums
falling from so many sprawling branches.
The blood in my glass has turned
to wine, dry with hints of spice. The flesh
on my table has turned to bread,
and it is good. I wash the red spot
from my palm, on which there is no wound.
I pull the chair back to the edge
of the table and sit, dip the bread in olive oil,
sip the wine, and I know that I have lost
nothing. That light in the night sky outside
my window is no beacon, only a star,
and by the time I can see it,
it has already burned to dust.

Creation Story
Jacquelyn Barnes

Over the earth, swaddled
in white, the spider woman, expert
weaver, and the Sun
in unison chant the magic
words to bring their diorama to life.

In the lonely underworld, she formed
the animals of clay and squeezed
their inanimate bodies into the cracks
between heaven and hell.

No sooner is the chant ended
the spider woman conceives of
humanity. As she sculpts the earthly
forms, she thinks to herself, *These
will be much harder to wake.*

To see deeper into you

Jacquelyn Barnes

To see deeper into you you say
that is why you want to read
and discuss poetry with me
to know the character of my
heart by the way it bounces
off another as you listen
you're building a safe home
for my sensitive heart though
it often senses wrongly. *Do not
wound yourself in him*, I repeat.
I will have to watch what I say,
for it cannot be unsaid. Even
here, in this house, where
the ears are generous.

The River People

Polly Buckingham

The river people sleep floating
in their basements. Birth

happens every night.
Their grass homes never burn,
but shine.

Killings do not change
the dreaming and floating.

The impervious river people
clap their green hands.

Hey diddle diddle
the rat stole the fiddle
but the party marches on.

Comets turn to stars
and stars to comets
and counting always goes wrong.

The river people wear their green
hats like crowns.

The river is grim
and still the river people
hang their green jackets to dry.

Turn them inside out
and turn them outside in,
the river people

are the shine in a dead man's eye.

The Last Day of January
Polly Buckingham

I visit the amphitheatre
at Morbid Pond. The ground is gauzy with snow's
left over netting. Red limber trees circle us.

I sit on one of many logs, the theatre's
scattered benches. All around me small men
in black paper hats catcall and clapp. Morbid Pond

has shrunk to a disc of soft ice the size of a manhole.
Somebody's knocking but I won't open the door. The air,
thick and dizzy, smells of sap and leaves.

There is no program, the men wave nothing
but their hands. There is no beginning of this show
that isn't. There's only an end.

Watching Men Outside My Apartment

Libby Burnette

Men lope the sidewalks outside my apartment
Some move with urgency, bodies swinging, long in stride
their shorts hung low, billowing bright as circus tents
Some move as quiet dancers, intrepid mimes of low tide
The drawer where I keep my rent
is shallow, musty, unfit for sacred objects
This whole world is pit and parceled, stymied by lament
The church the rehab the corner store offer their effects

Back and forth, they move like vanishing ships
pressing to their lips sometimes a dark ambrosia
Inside their coats I believe hearts have dipped
                        under the folds of the sea

At daybreak, a late autumn fog encloses the hillside
A young woman emerges briefly and disappears, wedded to the fog, a
    movable bride

Sleight of Hand from
the Monroe Street Bridge

D.S. Butterworth

Maybe it's smoke from fires across
the state filling the distances we come
to take for granted finally convincing
us that clarity is presence not absence,
or maybe the disclosure of raspberries
under the leaves from any shift
in memory's perspective, or the yearning
for a storm each jet's climbing roar
conjures, maybe how everything
has the architecture of a magic trick:
pledge, turn, prestige. We accept
the rigged deck or hat as ordinary,
our eyes following the flourish
of silk scarf away from the tell,
we laugh at the false blush of failure
that rushes the conceal of leaping card
or coin to the ultimate reveal. Maybe we
should have faith in some unseen
intelligence, like lungs and heart doing
their work without our directing,
even if we find out we believed
what we wanted all along despite
evidence to the contrary,
like those oxygen-starved climbers
who forget to turn around in time
to survive the descent, or the freezing
skiers who enter hot springs
only to ensure their hypothermia,
or the convalescent who convinces
himself just a little soup will do the trick

as he deepens his own starvation.
From the Monroe Street Bridge
the reek of human stain blooms
toward morning, but shifting our gaze
to the river it tumbles away, *just like that*,
a trick of green turbulence spilling
through a magician's ragged sleeve.

The Roadside Nothing Vendor
Thom Caraway

He has no fruit to sell, no one dollar
videos. Under his summer umbrella,
he sits in an aluminum folding chair.
His sign says nothing, and people stop,
expecting nothing. He has no novels,
no trinkets or post cards. And also none
of the following: light bulbs, boxes,
trips to exotic lands, scrap lumber.
He has no cars to sell, no electric
razors, no seashells, no comic books.
He has no secrets to sell you, no gossip.
The old lady down the road, pushing her cat
in a baby stroller—he sells her nothing
as she walks past. The light turns green
and cars go by. He waves and smiles.

Last Wild

Thom Caraway

"The Bunny Hills" are what the local
kids always called it. There are no
bunnies. The ghosts of the rail-yard
it once was remain. The 30-foot piling,
Devil's Chair, once held the bridge
across the river. Billy's house
down the block, high and long,
was the slaughter-house,
hogs and cattle brought in
by boxcar. Over time, the lines
shifted to the south bank,
the bridge dismantled, and the ties
removed. What remained was earth
and stone, rail spikes and oil barrels.
For years, the kids of West Central
rode bikes and caught snakes there,
the bunny hills, thirty square blocks
of detritus, gophers, and ragweed.
Now dozers and shovels scrape away
the hills, push through new roads,
a thin carpet of blacktop,
and builders pitch their wooden tents
where trains once sat, where kids
ran free, the last wilderness in town.
There is a plan to put in a park.

Rustle Road
Aimee Cervenka

I drove past your street again today,
and instead of the gentle movement of leaves,
I thought of horse theft. Specifically,
the two horses on the other side
of the retention pond we used to watch over breakfast,
their morning abruptly interrupted by the rattle
of an unfamiliar trailer, a strange hand on their gate.
Content as they were, they would not call out,
but calmly lip the offered apple cores
as ropes were fastened around their necks.
But your street is lined with trees. I don't know why
all I can think about are those horses and thieves
and the way, in those days, we called beauty
anything not made of concrete.

Spill

Aimee Cervenka

I washed the gloves as if there were still fingers inside,
working my thumbs over each knuckle
with small circular motions.
Even then, it seemed silly, my wish
to mount them on the wall,
palms cupped, fingers unfolding outward

as if you might have offered
to catch the sunlight leaking to the floor.

North South

Rebecca Chadwell

looks like it is going to snow: better chop wood, draw some water, feed the animals, and check on the old man who lives up the hill. look over last years wool. find gloves. where's the shovel? have you outgrown your boots?

here, the orange glow of the desert could thaw self-reliance into a flaccid hail mary. there, religious winters would have had her painted in a coat, obscuring the flaming heart of the desert.

In The Jamieson Valley
(A Billy Goat, Full After Eating)
Matt Comi

Charlie Farwell crushes empty cans of Rolling Rock
between his hoof and the pine stump

who knows nothing about Charlie,
or whether or not it is nine o'clock or if
the sun is setting or if it is July.

In the squash patch:
the sprinkler going, and un-going.

In the kitchen:
hand-me-down appliances breaking and un-breaking.

In the hayloft: they (Charlie and Someone) are
both naked and covered in straw, mouths full of grain.

The barn door slid shut, latched from both sides.
The honey-sun low and oiling everything.
Nothing yet, but maybe something soon.

Having Never Hunted

Matt Comi

In third grade,
Mrs. Maddox tells me that Thomas Edison
invented the lightbulb.

But now I'm listening to the host of an NPR
talk show say that that was a lie.

Who to trust?

It is easy to imagine the blind:
the rumble seat from my dad's

1927 Chevrolet hidden behind cut hemlock
and the boy holding two apples and a box of one

hundred grain, sof point ammo.

Or maybe I am imagining winter in a city park,
and a birder, who is patient and bored
and knows nothing about loss.

Vibrations

Chris Cook

She is always alone.
I see her several times a week, though she has never seen me.
Her progress along the sidewalk on South Regal is straight,
despite having never used her white cane like the others,
who waggle and tap from side to side.
Instead, she scoots it in front of her,
like a turntable stylus locked into the groove of a vinyl record,
picking up the vibrations of the Earth.
I wonder which album the world has selected for her today,
and whether she likes the music.
I decide that she does, because whenever I see her,
she's smiling.

She never wears dark glasses, either.
I'm grateful for that,
because I can see that her lovely eyes are always directed
slightly to the side and heavenward.
I feel a pang of guilt for watching her.
I was taught that staring is impolite,
but I perversely wonder if it's still rude
if the person you're staring at will never know.
Of course it's still rude—
what the hell is wrong with me for even *thinking* something like that?

Today, her path to the store is safe despite all the snow.
The neighbors have kept the sidewalks clear.
It's bitter cold, yet she's wearing a flimsy windbreaker.
Something tells me it's intentional—that her other senses are so keen
that she enjoys feeling temperatures in a way that I cannot fathom.
With her bloodhound-like sense of smell,
does she like picking up the scent of those who've passed this way?
Does she enjoy the buzz rush of unspeakably spicy food?

Does she go to outdoor concerts and cozy up to the speaker tower
to get sent to oblivion?
Can she experience love more deeply than others?
And has anyone loved her?

While she was in the store, the unthinkable has happened:
a plow has passed by and covered her path home
with a tidal wave of brown rime.
The Earth's surface has opened up;
the underworld has disgorged its evil bile for her to try to navigate.
The apocalypse has come.
Ultimately, she discovers that the only way to walk home
is on the shoulder of the busy street that's been narrowed by all the snow,
against the flow of traffic.
Ironically, it's foggy and dark,
so all the drivers have been partially blinded.
The cars are going too fast for the ice underfoot.
They have no choice but to pass dangerously close to her.
I know all of this because I, too, am in the line of cars driving towards her.
As I approach, I issue a silent prayer and an apology
as my passenger side mirror passes within inches of her.
In that instant, I see that she's still looking
slightly to the side and heavenward,
and that, for the love of sweet screaming Jesus,
she is still smiling.

A little while later, I wonder if maybe I love her.

Manito

Beth Cooley

Seen from the ridge above the pond,
the swan is the topsail of a doomed yawl,
a man's dress shirt blown astray,
a canvas duffle bag, empty and snagged
on a hidden branch.

Sleek masked head arched forward and sunk,
it might be feeding on snails, but for the odd angle
of its wings, extended like a gymnast's arms,
unnaturally graceful.

Its tentative mate nudges with her beak.
Full grown cygnets circle wide,
a trio of baffled gray moons.
Rings ripple outward from the stiffening form
as mallards and wood ducks glide away.

Alone, the body gives nothing
of poem or dance.
It lists slowly,
heavy and mundane.

Seasonal

Beth Cooley

In the yard across the street
Joseph kneels at an angle in the rain,
as if searching for evidence.

Alone, he looks like one of the hunched
smokers outside House of Charity—
hollow, opaque with a light inside

that hasn't been turned on yet.
He's waiting for Mary in her blue
robe, pink night gown underneath,

who will arrive once the rain stops.
And maybe there will be an angel,
strung up in the dogwood tree.

The whole scene, complete with
Baby-in-a-box will coalesce, each plastic
figure on the lawn full of light.

Next door, a herd of white wire
deer twinkle and nod in slo-mo
to the same old Christmas medley.

Stille Nacht, heilige Nacht.
Post-solstice, we are climbing
out of winter's grave
one minute at a time.

On the Universal Tendency to Debasement in the Sphere of Love

Brian Cooney

Without a door, she gives up on correspondence, but translating her scars
into names for captive birds, she teaches herself Farsi anyway.

Observing the anniversary of her death, she bakes cookies she won't eat
and spends the morning weaving ravens out of weeds.

Her imaginary friend looks like a younger Freud. He never speaks, just
smokes
and watches dapper as her boy throws poems behind the settee

saying "live" or "die." The air is thick with wings: the huma, tormented
by absent sky, refuses to cast its shadow on a floor littered with feet.

Her fingers fall one at a time. Nothing in the room is real but the view.
She wonders if she'd get anywhere by lining them each to each.

Value

Linda Cooper

There is a yard sale at 7th and Cedar. Bring all your friends.
Books are fifty cents a box.

A man has died,
and his bookstore.
The books are barely breathing.

Every room is full,
books piled in uneven stacks,
some too high to reach.
They spill from their boxes,
arms open, ready for whatever
lives on after death:
the breath of stars,
the scent of intention,
floaters wading on the glass of an eye.

A sign says:
This is the last day.

A tall mirror bows to a young man
in a red hat. The books call out.
He places one hand on a stack
like a preacher
or a defendant.

He has been two hours,
in the fat green chair,
reading, while the dead man's
children wait in the shadows
for 3 o'clock,

when they'll
load up and drive
to the landfill.

It is one minute to three,
and the young man in the red hat
wants to say something.

Winter Driving in the Northwest
Mikayla Davis

The fields on either side are white
and blind and the sun breathes
into earth's ear
cold words, that send shivers
into the wind, but I

am warm, tucked tightly
into the seat of my car, pressed
too close to the drivers
around me, splattered
with the brown-gray slush,
like smeared mascara,
like a monochrome rainbow
arched across my windshield.

The snow, crushed
beneath my tires, sounds like fault
lines shifting, pulling right and left,
pushing me off the edge
and into the deceptive depths
of white on the side of the road

and the trees, with frosted boughs
weighed down by beauty,
like so many children
with their heads hung low,
reach out for closeness,
their backs breaking,
wood splintering,
at the warmth of metal's embrace
and they shed tears
of clarity.

Boxers

Tom I. Davis

Not one punch is landed in the dream
not only that but none is thrown. These bully
boys, encumbered by recent ingestion
of hair straightener, near overdoses

of pharmaceuticals not yet invented, know
the heavy bag in the gym as their mother
or at least a younger boy to punch out or ignore
beneath the klieg lights in despondency purposed.

These were the shorted-out fellas, the half boys,
beleaguered into indemnity of diminishment,
not crazed nor gruesome and tragic, just left out,
the cost of it all, futile in the dream.

Tonight they're being taught the art of
fisticuffs, the idea that at least what we are
matters even battered with haymaker eyebrows
above that dizzy glare goats on oats wear.

Life
Tom I. Davis

Tiny twitters darting in and out
amongst the cottonwood foliage
chirruping in a most elegant tone
while on the north shore three
mergansers hold lackadaisically
in the backwash. Downstream
a dozen geese emit a strong hullo
then are off the water streaming
in a six-to-a-wing goose formation
over my head squawking code
deliriously and deliriously I am
eased into my faint role of nothing
but color, churn and slap of water,
morning light streaming under
the bridge above the waterfall
and each particle of my being
and non-being holds knowing
of your being, of your benevolence
in spite of everything loving me.

True Love in the Bushes

Tom I. Davis

I love best the knocked down, roughed up
empty natural places in our city where no foot
but mine has entered, ever, from before
time even before nurture was needed as a verb.

On voting day the indenture to ill-considered
caring is mediated in the meat grinder,
a harlequin demagogue of belief about faith
when all it is is a tight grip and a loose lip
naming joy "joy" or managing a small family

and the city wells up with 200-foot pine
throughout all the city out into Idaho
now and then a church spire, a government
building, a water tower but mainly the pines
and the calming mountain on the horizon.

Gold Watch

Krista Marie DeBehnke

I counted the year by months and weather patterns
because you took my only gold watch
and skipped Spokane for bigger mountains
and the new breath of a dark-haired girl.
We've come full circle back to July
and I think you took the breeze, too,
and left dry, stagnant air
that won't leave—an orphaned bird
who returns to a familiar branch
hoping for nostalgia long gone.
You thief, you wolf,
you took my only gold watch
and any fond memory of summer
and any reason for me to stay
so I'll steal the last thing you own—
me in this city,
I'll move south
to a place I'd never go
so you can't picture me there
or here
because I'm gone.

When Petals Fall

James Decay

She's in the kitchen, crying
red petals
falling around her feet
from a vase
of wild tulips
we picked together

She asks
if I know
what it is
to lose something
I've held dear

I tell her
of a day I sat
in an alley
staring upward
at snowflakes
falling between
brick buildings
begging God
to spare the friend
wrapped in my arms
as his life escaped
in heartbeats
from a stab wound
on his neck

She wipes
her cheek
and says

I wonder
if flowers beg
when their petals
fall from the stem

Dick Schofield is Not a Metaphor

Jeffrey G. Dodd

My daughter loves Dick Schofield.
You remember Dick? Light-hitting
shortstop for the Angels. Dick,

who surely spent his boy years
dreaming ways to be like his dad,
Ducky, not an actual or imagined

duck, but a real to life World Series
Champion. She clutches him tight,
nibbling his corners, biting the bill

of his baseball cap. She doesn't love
Dann Bilardello this way. Or Mackey
Sasser, or any of the players whose

names captured my youth in their
gravitational suck. Or little Bip Roberts
who had very little bip in his bat. Or,

even, Glenn Davis, who in my tenth
summer hit enough home runs to push
the Astrodome's narrow orbit off its tilt.

Oh, Glenn Davis, the Big Bopper, bopping
the Space City's hopes into the stratosphere
and beyond, only to see his team fall

short in October's gaunt gloom. Those were
rough times in the Fall of '86. The Talking
Heads teaching me through the speakers

of my brother's restored Comet that this
was the same as it ever was, and me not
wanting to believe that life would be

an endless loop of Craig Reynolds playing
his best Neil Armstrong and stepping
safely onto the dimpled face of first

base, the umpire calling him out again
and again. But this is my burden,
Or one of them, and it's lighter now.

Hers will be her own, I know, and may
have nothing to do with Dick Schofield,
but her love for close-shorn, steady

Dick Schofield says much about my girl's
character, her interest in steadfast love,
her firm moorings as she crawls the living

room with Dick Schofield between her
thin teeth. It is important that she chose
him among the hundreds of mostly

forgotten players' cards my mother
packed haphazardly in a box which
she then meticulously wrapped in three

layers of shipping tape before sending
the whole chaw-spitting, crotch-shifting
lot on a two thousand mile sprint

around the bases and onto my home's
front steps two days before my daughter
fell in love with Dick Schofield, along

with a note: "Maybe these are worth
something." Dick Schofield, I want
to tell my mother, is worth something.

The Hitchhiker
Michelle Bonczek Evory

I erased you at mile 251.
Just pushed the mile counter and Poof,
you were gone. Like that. Zero. Not even a snowflake
on the car's warm rug. Not even an eyelash
mite. Earlier, we braked for a tabby
crossing the road and laughed. We licked
enchiladas from the crescent moons
of each others' chins. I might miss the taste
of your smoky breath, might think again of
your pale blue eyes, an unsure December sky,
your fingers, my waist, your thumb
on my hip bone, your unshaven face. How you told me
I was beautiful, how you told me you were willing
to stick all the way to the coast. Willing to ride
west, feed my tank gas, be Amazon
in the Olympics, be Boa Constrictor
in the Hoh. Take my picture
with my mouth around the horn of a mountain goat.
And all that was swell. Hell, no one
had ever offered to carry my bags
miles through the woods for some peace
and fire, maybe some s'mores. Too bad.
We could've melted together
like chocolate mousse on a hot tongue, cream
and eggs, baby. Cream and eggs. We could've held each other
steady on each others' shoulders. But I erased you
at mile 251, not even a dent from our last destination,
not even a full tank of gas gone.

The Birds on the Prairie

Lauren Gilmore

The birds on the prairie are dropping
like flies. From one of their collapsed frames,
pushed hastily to the side of the street,
a rolled-back pair of beady eyes
look up at me, seeming to understand
what they have lost. Around them
grey blocks of cookie-cutter neighborhoods
are spreading like cancer. I remember
when the metal jaws of construction crews first
started tearing up the ground to build them.
Dad used to take us to the open houses,
let us walk our fingers along the
marble countertops, while he acted interested
and full of questions, an empty leather
bound wallet burning a hole
in his pocket. I'd look out at the price
on the sign with the real estate agent's picture
and count how many zeroes it had,
so I could report back to him later, ask what
number that made it. Above the small
tight-fenced yards, telephone lines
crisscrossed through white clouds, like an
unfinished game of connect the dots.
Dad would lift me up onto his shoulders when
it was time to go. I'd put my palms onto
his balding head, pretending to steer him
like a ship crossing the Atlantic.

Closing the Fuel Station

Lindsay Golden

Everything smells of gasoline
coming home
I rolled my windows down
and sacrificed my thoughts
to the rain.

My pants are still wet.

Audrey
Isaac Grambo

Standing in the back row
of a chaotic poetry slam
in the middle of a three-story
art party, Audrey taps my shoulder
and smiles into my face
like a four year-old who
knows where the cookies are hidden.

It is the third day of an
international event in our
home city, and I am sleep deprived
and she is drunk, giddily
stomping around in her
trademark black leather jacket.

"Isaac, I am so happy right now!"
she says, and she hugs me
for an eternity.

This hug

Is 100 tons of relief and desperation;
of pride and panic;
of self-loathing pathos;
and spit-shined Doc Martens.

Her smile is as wide as the sky
and her eyes are bright beams of light
but her hug is as many shades as her
hair color. We have fifteen conversations
in a single embrace.

Audrey is the strongest, toughest girl
you're gonna run into in Peaceful Valley,
and she'll tell you what she thinks before
you ask; before she even thinks it.

She's going to leave this town—
go to Seattle or The Bay or Peru.
She's going to stay right here—
build it into the powerhouse
she knows she deserves.

When you're nineteen,
nothing in this city makes sense;
nobody listens to what you believe in
even as you're screaming it in their face.

When you're nineteen,
everything in this city makes sense;
its bifurcated self-image reflects your shattered
understanding of your own beliefs
as it screams them into your face.

Outside Tenth Street Station, I sat on a curb
and got drunk. I wrote a love poem
to a city I had no choice but to leave.
Knees in the gutter, I knew
the only place I could go
to feel at home again was Spokane.

Outside The Baby Bar, Audrey sits on the curb
and smokes a cigarette. Her hair is bleach-brass
with blue tips and her fingernails are black but chipped.
The ever-present black leather jacket combines
with her posturing of worldly disdain to ward off
the well-wishers scouring the gutters.

She sees me from half a block away and she
transforms into that giddy four year-old again.
She calls my name and stands up to wait for me.
We have seventy-three conversations in a single embrace.

We are two hearts separated by fifteen years
and eight thousand miles.

We are one soul holding an entire city in the sky.

Wallace, Where God Lives in Silver
Michael Gray

Say you found God here,
stashed in mortar between
cracked ice on frozen concrete steps
below a punched-through sign filled
with wind and falling snow. Or
in ore chunks and antique tools
and the old rail depot, its tracks consumed in road,
that summons tourists to roam bordello rooms.
Here is silver. Here it bleeds.
More fish sicken, gills swelled, filling
the Coeur d'Alene, and burn
birds' lungs with metal silt.
You prefer another town,
some other streets.

Spokane, maybe, where city buses run past
eight, and snowplows crumble new
flakes. Freight trains echo, rumbling
by old snow crusts like dying
embers or dirty streaks of God flung
like ore in pans. He's found in gritty
silt, or Geiger runways, inhaled
by waiting Bombardiers. In Wallace,

St. Ignatius contemplates
by the basketball hoop, under I-90's
passing trucks. He might think
of silver. Mine for chunks. Veins
of cars and piled cairns of ice still
hum, holy as spun earth.

The Long Nights
Timothy Greenup

I miss my friend Brent from Southern California. I planned to never miss
anything from Southern California. Yet, here I am, at our coffee shop,
watching the door.

The door is an image that crops up often in dreams of those who feel,
for one reason or another, trapped in life.

There's life, Tim, says the gypsy dishwasher of the fried chicken restaurant
I work when I'm sixteen, and then there's life! He tugs at his crotch.

Somewhere surgeons botch a surgery, minnows swim blindly into the mouth
of something ugly.

On my bed, sixteen again, I listen to terrible choruses—I dig in my belly
button for films or cheeses. Finger smells of something—crematorium,
Gorgonzola. Forests of eyebrows

fighting vainly
against the flames. A tattoo inside my forearm I didn't ask for.
After walking around

outside all night, I return home and find my torso steaming, my feet cold
but, strangely, sweating.

Mother's going to be so mad at me.

The Realization

Timothy Greenup

Neighborhood graying from change.
Crows lift, confidently, onto
power lines and call familiar
names. In a far window, a cat
grows angry.
All that movement and defiance,
others are bound to be intrigued
and join in. And what then? If all
take to the sky, poor terror
gets lonely, bored, and dies.

And There Was Some Confusion

Tom Gribble

I'd not seen my sister Darlene cry that hard
since Leroy Swaney fell fifteen stories
from a window-washer's scaffold in Washington D.C.
He was dead long before the Heard Standard told us
that a local football star was killed.
And there was some confusion in the news
as to whether he'd jumped, was pushed
or something simple had broken.

I asked my sister why.
She said, "Someone in Dallas shot the President."
We gathered around the black and white TV,
a nascent Vietnam reports slipped into the background.
Walter Cronkite, CBS celebrant,
held his horn-rims held like a Sanctus bell
and brought the news,
"President Kennedy died at 1:00 p.m. Central Standard Time."
I left in the repeat.

Cool Spring was a long street
that came then left the city in straights and turns
houses rowed elbow to elbow in town,
but as street ran north, there was more room
between lives to breathe.

I sat on a wall three feet high.
It was once steady but weather cracks weakened
and in places the wall simply gave up.
I didn't stay long. The concrete became cold
after the sun rolled down Besson Hill
like it was a child's ball slipped from fingers
not used to holding that roundness.

I passed Joe Hartoe on my way home.
"Mister Hartoe," I said
not allowed to call him a name as ordinary as Joe.
"It's too bad about President Kennedy, ain't it?"
He rubbed his hands over his eyes, over his mouth
like he washed his face with the night.
"Yes," he said without losing his walk.
He was the first man I'd seen cry.

Our all-American family left for D.C. the day before the funeral.
We climbed the Summit Mountain toward Cumberland Gap.
Five p.m. grayed our windows.
Road signs at each cross on U.S. 40
Stacked like geographical totems,

Chalk Hill, Fort Necessity, Hagerstown.
The radio blurted on with fickle clarity.
A bulletin said the assassin had been killed,
and there was some confusion
on how to feel about the homicide.
I dozed off in the palm of the backseat.

Before dawn we stopped at a neon oasis
in the black of Indian Springs.
I put cream and sugar in coffee
and drank from a cup with the heft of stone, dull white
and rounded at the top to fit anyone's lips.
From the jukebox's speaker

came the banjo haunt of Washington Square.
The music cut through the orders for ham and eggs.
I held the rhythm in my head
and played it long after the nickel song was done.

I watched the electric orange CAFÉ sign
shrink to a speck in car's rear window
then a bend in the road took it completely.

The knots in the road or the radio finding air to be loud
were the only hints that time was moving at all.

D.C. stretched out to meet us
in a montage of stark whites and ghetto-plexes.
We neared the Capitol mall,
the streets were insane with people. Our family held hands
hooked together like a child's big block train.
We sifted with thousands of others
Between marble monuments built for national postcards.

We doubled our blankets against the cold and sat down
huddled in Monday. The gathered in their talking,
their whispering, and usual breathing
howled in the canyon of granite.
Without warning a quiet spilled over us.
There was the hollow of seashell held to an ear.
A soldier sat a white horse, six more white ones
pulled the caisson with the casket draped.
The President's brothers, sultans of image, walked cadence.

There was a chill for my spine
in the one-beat-time of a slow drum coming.
There were polished boots backwards in silver stirrups.
And there was some confusion
in the eyes of the rider-less Black Jack
as the horse reared its huge head.
We watched its prance until it faded into yesterday.

Lilies, Stones, Glass

Iris Gribble-Neal

for Tom Davis

He said he wasn't really a tough guy, but you
already know that by the blue flock of surrender
flying from his eyes. He just leaned a little
too far into history and can't get back,
swinging from his grandfather's watch
fob, a trapeze artist of wavering doubt.
He keeps counting his legs, *one, two,*
one, two, knows if he stays too long
lichen will grow from his torso like trees.

So you never really killed anyone, you tell him.
Your bones still push against skin trying to get out.
You still wander old highways of the heart as if they are
silk roads whispering the streets of ghost towns.

His eyes become interrupted by broken things:
lilies, stones, glass, from a distance
they're all the same. History crouches
on the porch, a gargoyle
keeping his luck in or out
depending on which train travels
the cinder tracks through his dusty past,
whistling from the soft throats of women.

Playing the Horses

Iris Gribble-Neal

I'll see your horse and call with a minor herd
stretching the horizon with long necks,
manes flowing into wispy wings.
I believe in hooves beating
dub-dub, dub-dub like drums of a heart.

Oh, you'll cry all right, but no one will
hear because of the geese downriver
muttering like old men in John Deere hats
about weather and the price of wheat.
You'll be sorry you lost the horses,
one bad debt after another piling up,
a dark enigma in the corner
rich with dust and cat hair,
dead bugs all legs up. It doesn't matter
how much tequila you spill;
it's not like salt and no one's coming
to dinner while silence
drips in the night like a faucet.
You're stuck there with the gypsy
fortune teller, your heart as red
as Georgia in her palm.

Fledge

Emily Gwinn

> *I think he'll be to Rome*
> *As is the osprey to the fish, who takes it*
> *By sovereignty of nature.*
>
> William Shakespeare, Coriolanus: *Act 4, scene 7*

You cannot speak to the osprey,
the osprey will speak to you
when ready,
in daydream,
in sunlight pressing open a river,
splitting seams
into memory
of pikeminnow,
bridgelip sucker
and ultrasound.

Fish spin their soft bodies
into golden coins,
leap from rivers into talon,
giving themselves over
as offerings to their god.

The osprey takes
what it wants.

This morning
high above the trail,
an egg hatches,
cracking wide into
sea hawk, fish eagle, raptor,
a diurnal heartbeat
of cloud.

It is quiet below
the nest,
quiet in this hollow body.
I hold my breath
against wind,
push hard against

the changing season.

It will be weeks before
a soft, brown tuft of chick
will appear from the edge
of basket, months before
it will tip it's own weight
against sky,
but already there is expectation,
a learning of balance
and gravity,
where one egg cracks wide,
another will remain,
motionless.

The osprey knows
what to keep.

Unlike this fruitless body
which holds nothing:
no chick, no bone,
no seed
or slick scale of minnow.
I linger under the nest
waiting for a sign,
a signal of recognition,
for the osprey to finally
open her wings
and carry me home.

Spokane

Elizabeth Hansen

Who are these people
lining the streets
going about their business?
I do not know them,
they do not know me,
and yet we are brethren.
They come and they go,
some sketchy, some pretty
some known, some unknown.
Walking past
these ancient buildings
whose stories are sometimes forgotten.
They do not know
the memories, the stories
made on these very streets.
They do not know
the past behind the eyes
of every one they see.
They yell and they fight
if something displeases them.
They avoid and they dodge
if someone strikes fear in them.
They do not know
that this person is the same
they saw as a child
as they played together on the red wagon.
They do not know
that this person shares the memory
of feeding ducks down by the river.
They both saw the same parade,
the same bands marching the same streets.
This city is old,

with many memories, many stories,
as the old paint chips
and the neighborhoods remain divided.
Perhaps it could be better,
perhaps it could improve,
but this city is my home,
and I wouldn't choose any other.

Songs to Summer—
Four Movements

Stine Hansen

I.
Smoking yellow pills
  on the banks of the river
    all the world ablaze

Empty the fly trap,
  then turn your thoughts to ice cream.
    Antiemetic

Drowning out traffic,
  the rattle of training wheels
    just before bedtime.

II.
Nasturtium, dearest
  with your contortionist stems.
    So adaptable!

Striped like melons;
  clinging hard to the screen door.
    June beetles, July.

Grey, hazy, sunset.
  Missionaries pedal by,
    balancing, hands free.

III.
The bee falls asleep
   deep inside a squash blossom—
      intoxicated.

Late into Spring we
   harvested Claytonia.
      Seems like years ago.

Farewell to phonebooths.
   Farewell typewriters, mix-tapes,
      cursive love letters.

IV.
Slipshod in sweatpants—
   it's not a fashion statement,
      it's a way of life.

Remember Summer.
   Remember cucumber barbs
      and green bean velvet.

Scent of wet asphalt,
   pine needles, puffballs. Midday,
      the river recedes.

Spokane Triptych
Dennis Held

1. Spokane Is My Boss

I work for Spokane and it hurts,
tires me out digging all that basalt
and raw splendor tossed away
wears me down that damned river
all day every day going and going
away all the time, even at night
and the pay sucks because there's
always unskilled laborers like me
who will do it for a little less because
we have mouths to feed and hell
we'd pay Spokane to let us stay
and keep working because everything
is so broken but it's our job
to fix it because there's no one
around to hand it to because they're
already busy repairing the one bridge
we're all standing on far from shore
so no one can leave because it's
a full-time job just staying alive
in Spokane.

2. Spokanefish

There's a reason they're not called game fish:
they're rough fish, and there's no bag limit.
If you catch a Spokanefish you'll want to
throw it back: huge scales all over with too
many bones to eat it and odd fins where
there should not be fins and a big sucker
mouth on the underside of its oversized

bottomfeeding head and barbells like
a catfish that sting, scientists say
don't eat them because of heavy metals
and some people curse them and throw
them on the bank to die but they don't—
they suck in enough air to crawl back
to the river on that weird set of extra
fins because you can't kill a Spokanefish
with just one whack.

3. Girlfriend

Spokane is my girlfriend and she spits
and belches and farts and says "motherfucker"
in a way that insults both mothers and fuckers
but she never says she's sorry or calls me
honey anymore and she needs a hot bath
and eats crappy fast food and smokes
rolled-up shwag leaf all day and drives
a rusted out eighty-four Datsun pickup
with no spare tire and she calls me drunk
on her ass at three in the morning saying
baby come over I need a piece of your ass
and I say no way and she says honey I am
so sorry and so what can I do?
I get up and go see Spokane.

At the Bottom of the Ocean

Kimiko Hirota

The year is ending
but I do not know that yet.
Lying dormant
at the bottom of the ocean
I could not tell you
the difference
between night and day.
There is darkness
called water,
called safety blanket,
my hair heavy and tangled
but not resting on my back.
It is floating
as I sink onto rock and sand.

A squid rests his tentacles
on my feet, becoming
a new friend.
My world is so quiet
with density,
a surround-sound of nothing
and it is magic.
Thoughts of light trickle
in between
wrinkled fingers
but I do not miss my heart
that once raced
with every smile
that touched it.

Today it beats
slow, weightless.

Dust does not exist
at the bottom of the ocean.
Wounds heal with salt water
and the kisses from seaweed
are enough to grieve
a body cold.

Fragments

Jackson Holbert

I

We dipped our shoulders beneath the heat and found whiskey in the earth. Cars passed. Passengers stared. And still darkness eased its way across the scabland. And still we persisted.

II

Grandma, dead at eighty of emphysema, who scoured the reservoirs for arrowheads, speaks, tells me "no, no, only the penny slots, don't want them Indians too rich now, do we boy?" I see her dry waterfall of a face in the cheap pine coffin her sons were too weak or fat to lower on their own.

III

Uncle George (Custer), dead at eighteen, nineteen, twenty-one, twenty-two, twenty-three, twenty-eight, thirty-three, forty-one and fifty-nine—who, with Coyote (a friend of his who, after his wife kicked him out, stayed in a motor home by George's double-wide for eight years) once took me hunting with a water-cooled machine gun—lights up the sky with three thousand dollars worth of fireworks every Fourth. I hear gravy drip from his beard, his mouth open, teeth all awry. His truck has no brake shoes; he says he'll fix them when the emergency wears out.

IV

Every September the air would gasp beneath the bluegrass burns of Idaho. They're illegal now. There's a feeling they—used to—give me. The way fires dove past the seeds, trying to find something deeper in the soil. The way the coffee-stained horizon coughed up bits of darkness. The way smoke, made of so many small machines, so many moving parts, leaked light.

A Party on the Way to Rome
Christopher Howell

In rouge of the night lanterns
I saw four of them rise, one trailing
a blanket, and steal to a bunk near
where I pretended sleep.
Beyond bulkheads and decks the sea
was a rushing dirge by which they cast
that blanket over the man there and began
to hit, hissing "How's this you fucking
faggot shit!"

Most of us little more than boys, taken off
to war in the usual way, lay listening
to the curses and the cries.

When they were done, Chuck, the leader, saw me
watching and could not clear his face of angry, shamed
confusion, a man caught between what was
and what was wrong. Meanwhile
the beaten one began to scream, "You let them
do it, you just let them!" Then he went weeping
and bleeding up the ladder, the compartment behind him
quiet as a burned out church.

When the MAA, taking his time, came among us,
his flashlight could not wake a single witness
so he left, shrugging, promising Justice.

Aeneas endured the distant smoke he knew was Dido
burning. *Poor wench.* But nothing could sway him
from the path appointed. That is, the free
right life, even the very fruits of empire, was not
so far or difficult to reach, we knew, if one held

steady, unnoticed and on course, if one obeyed
necessity's goddess and could pay
with the kind of fear that pleased her. So smoke
drifted

beyond horizon's palpable secret and nothing more
came of it. So on our very own ship a man
had dared not to sail from whatever called him
master of the undivided self.
So he had loved men,
it was more than you could say
for the rest of us.

First Touch

Christopher Howell

After the movie, the garden golf,
coffee, and long soulful walk,
after the alternating daisy petals
of elation dejection elation, we stood
in the klieg lights on her front porch.
I could hear through the door
the ox-like breathing of her father
poised to fling it wide and pounce.
From the roundness of her green eyes
I could tell she heard it too.

But inside us some kind of execution
was on the way, and we were its last meal,
our mouths beginning to know this
and to open, slightly and drift toward each other
like clouds.

We had been kissing for months.
This kiss was not that
country, this one
had nothing to do with gratitude
or the sort of evening we had had
or expectation
or revenge against parents and the church
or even curiosity.
It was the exclusivity of desire, the dizzy
mutually sudden focus of our young neurons
driving us onto a single unrepeatable moment
of physical revelation fused to a steam
of lips and tongues and interpenetrating breath.

When at last we disengaged from that
eternity, still

holding me, she turned her back to the door, took
my hand and, in a gesture ceremonially exact, placed it
upon her breast.
She was wearing a bra, a blouse, a sweater
and a coat. She might have been Joan of Arc
arrayed for battle.
Nevertheless, the magnitude of this gift
surged up my arm, neck, and into my hair
till I began to lift
or faint
and felt the moon raking my blood with gems.

She drew away, smiled a little, and opened the door.
Her father, standing like Stonehenge
against the living room light, allowed her in
then shut the whole house, hard, the lion-headed
brass knocker banging like a gunshot.

I moved throbbingly down the steps and headed home.
After a block or so I could walk
normally. The softness of her lips and tongue,
that roundness and tension beneath my palm
as she held it to her, every step
brought these and such a warm loneliness
came over me, I thought I would not much mind death
then, if gods *could* die.

I walked down Hawthorn Street from 82nd to 89th
through a hall of overhanging trees, through the small
kivas of light that fell from the streetlamps.
Did I continue on Hawthorn to 92nd
or turn left and cross the dark school yard?
It was a long time ago. Kennedy was President; Viet Nam
just a place we sent "Advisors."
Moths were circling the porch lights and dying
in ecstasies of brilliance.
No one in the world but her
knew where I was.

Untitled

Kristine Iredale

Walking under moonlight
across the base.
We come across three Iraqis.
Spotting them
some hundred meters away.
The tallest is the same height
as the both of us.
While the shortest one
wears a large jacket
and none wear the badge
they must wear
once inside the base.
We place our hands
more firmly
on our rifles
as my buddy yells,
"Where's your fucking badge."
They stop abruptly
like they just hit a wall.
The shortest man
puts his hand
inside his large jacket
pulling out a badge.
I can see the trembling
in his hands
and I think to myself.
So this is what it's like
to play God.

Lucky

Kristine Iredale

Miss! Miss!
Captain Edwards says we're the same age.
Your birthday is only two weeks before mine.
I've been learning English
since the beginning of the war
from the soldiers that pass through here.
I make a good living as an interpreter.
I can take care of you.
Just give me your father's email address
so we can settle on the dowry.
I'll offer him two thousand US dollars,
two goats, and a camel.
He gets down on one knee
tells me I have the most beautiful blue eyes.
I respond yes
I get them from my father
and he's not giving his little girl away to you.
He tells me
I should feel lucky
most women aren't worth
anything at all.

Sprague Walker

Mischa Jakupcak

How can I carry snapshots of crime scenes
& splinters from high beams
that crack overhead from below?

Pushing weary feet onwards
over highways & backroads
when I know this life
is a teetering mechanical monster,
a crippled dinosaur mountain.

It's all a dangerous ramshackle fake.

An orange & green duct-taped disaster
gasping its very last breath.

Eager to fall to the wayside
leaving all its lost parts
in shopping mall bathrooms
& motel parking lots
in greasy, blue alleys
on the other side of the state.

Yesterday's second place prizes
trophies and tokens
get dusty and broken
& forgotten in corners
like me.

You might just as well live.

So share in this brightness,
or leave with your lightness.

Much better now
be warned.

Lets get it all over
let me break all the lanterns
as if each was my lonely, last toy.

Its what I know in history & hysteria
well worn pages

Repetition breeds repeating again

Laugh hollow laughs
with the crowd as they get their fair share
& their moment to dance in the sun.

I am still
that lost child
limping & whining

a l o n e

with the prayers of kind strangers,
smothered by darkness
bleeding, freezing, pleading
for home.

Walking Spokane to Ritzville

Jonathan Johnson

Forget the Lincoln who won't give an inch
when you've walked the shoulder into days
of horizon to get to this sage and few
sunflowers, bare sky and desiccated fence posts.
In the long between time consider instead
the soul at the throttle of the orange engine
before the train you can't see the end of.
How your slow, tired wave came back as two blasts.
Remember this morning's single goldfinch,
which rose from low willow to power line
over your passing. The uncountable sparrows
crowding barb wire and power lines later.
Crowding your sky. A high, faint contrail.
Remember six miles back where this two-lane
crossed the interstate, a nothing junction
for which you'd waited anyway as somewhere
to peel your tin of sardines and drink your last
water, the sign that rose instead, a silhouette
from the hot end of sight, and twenty hopeful
minutes later read, yes, *Restaurant*.
If the cross hanging at the chest of the gaunt
waitress who brought you your four over-easies
with whatever cheese they had and chocolate shake
was also nothing to you, later when it hung
again at the chest of her daughter who came
(I swear) on crutches from behind the counter
and asked if she could help put out silverware
it shone in your tired sentimentality
and the sun down through tall glass behind you.
If that grace was easy, take it anyway.
When the mother filled your bottles from the tap
and offered ice and her smile showed the gap
where a tooth had gone, you could never imagine

what you'd need far into more land alone
when another scarce car took so long toward you
and leaned into your path and slowed, a grill-less
Lumina, and you almost reached for the black can
of pepper spray that hung from your belt a warning
against just such a moment. But it was her.
The mother. She remembered your wide hat.
Your water bottles. So now you must remember
the ride she offered to the next far town.
That she was willowy and younger than you
and you would never have called her beautiful,
standing and squinting with her cross in the smell
of cut wheat and asphalt baked gray
by some thousand days of blank sun. Remember
that when you thanked her anyway you were
both, but for the other, unwitnessed. You said
you were walking. She said okay. It's good
to get some exercise. You must hold this.
Hold the dusty blue back of her car long
after it's gone into more hot hours alone.
Hold the exquisite emptiness into which
your life has put rocks. Fence. Tar-veined highway.
Hurt inside your boots. Tick of a grasshopper
tumbling onto the road. Hold the vastness
and the first breeze turning afternoon evening
that draws forth your kindness. So when the white Ram
veers his loud, fast tires over the line
towards you and you edge farther down onto
gravel then weeds and he veers yet closer
you can think—later—not of the pebbles
you could have tossed up in his windshield's path,
nor of the can of pepper spray in your grip,
but—in the quiet again—of the water
arcing in low sunlight over tall hay.
Think of the waitress' child's cross, if you must.
Think of the man in the truck as a boy.
And of the town those trees and silo mean
must be close by. And think of the father.
The slap, slap, slap reverberating still.

Proving Ground

Aileen Keown Vaux

A giant squid appears below the research vessel,
tentacles sluicing through black water
toward the electronic bait.

The monster avoids small prey,
and attacks above the undulating light
hopeful for bigger game to satisfy its appetite.

Brother, you always believed
in creatures who hid
in forests and underwater canyons.

When you left what did you believe
would wait for you on wooded trails,
in the frost-furred ridge?

Sasquatch lives, you say, a beast who swings
branches against thick trunks,
a solid crack that rings across the Cascade,
a call I cannot stop, a call you run toward.

Here to Learn the Sport of Fishing, I Ask to Work the Line

Aileen Keown Vaux

hook live bait while we talk the habits of small-mouth bass,
mimicking the men who glide easy in Pond Oreille.

Up-river my uncle tends his trailer park lawn.
He is a silver fox mowing through the scenery after divorce,

proposing an explanation for his marriage will, one day,
float belly-up in the river.

Sometimes fishing happens in the absence water
when so much depends on a good story told in the quickening night.

If I were honest, he says,
I fall asleep, most nights, sitting upright in my camping chair.

But that's not the story he and I were taught
by family habit to relay; here are too many sharp edges, dusty with defeat.

I'll finish for him instead: last night, lured by the firelight,
we sat beneath the sky: a dusting of stars like sugar on a midnight table.

Blazing New Trails on the Fire Lane
Scott Kinder-Pyle

Before my fatal heart attack I blaze around the cul-de-sac
and walk upon the trail. The wetlands there are frail
with run-off from each roof. And I wish I were aloof,
like water fowl, to damage. But what's the old adage?
A bird in hand is worth more than a land's reclamation?
Asymmetric ripples scroll eclectic marquees in June.
A woman joins me soon who turns an even fifty.
She's always been thrifty; and Wednesday's no exception
to her predilection: *I hope the farmer never sells...*
Does that ring any bells? We bisect cattails and wheat
with barns and tractors' conceit. And we're supposing
this trail's for hosing down our houses in flame.
And so catastrophe's to blame for meadows so paved.
(A hook & ladder might save for no other reason.)
But now's the season to let belongings burn. Out of
compulsion, before we turn, we discern which to spurn.

Thinking About John G. Lake's Grave

Laurie Klein

> *Rev. Lake, through divine healing, has made*
> *Spokane, WA, the healthiest city in the world.*
> *—circa 1915 report, Washington D. C.*

Call my disease wind-in-a-pine,
rocking me, crown to root.
Misfired nerves and synapses
mutiny, crippling toes while,

evergreen, your prayers
spill, crisp as those aging needles
overhanging Lake's grave, latent
acid amending clay,

little mounds of death
festooning a modest plot where
the faithful gather. Believing
a dream for these feet, forlorn

as a pair of rats deserting a ship,
your talismans come,
laid in the fold of an earnest note—
to burn or steep, or take and eat?

Your tendered hope
elicits laughter, trumped
by shame. Later I'll wonder: magic,
or miracle? This remission.

Women and Children First

Leyna Krow

I

The second largest city in Washington State
holds its breath until 8 p.m. on
August nights when it finally
exhales long shadows that make even
shirtless men on front steps,
half-bare pine trees, cats with no tails
look still and golden and new.

II

My boyfriend and I have suspicions
about the businesses on Northwest
Boulevard. We believe they are not what
their signs say. The tattoo parlor is really
a whorehouse. The barbershop is
really a tattoo parlor. The hardware store
carries hammers, but no nails.

III

In the fall, everyone in town
drives north to pick apples and pumpkins and breathe heavy,
damp air that hangs out in front of their mouths
like a threat. The sun, a dim lamp with an energy-saving bulb.
Small boys scale hay bales and jump
with arms forward like tiny Supermen,
determined to do only good.

IV
The neighbor girl, who is seven,
tells us that for the school harvest play,
she's been assigned the role of the elephant,
which she rightfully suspects
is not a traditional harvest animal.
But it's less degrading than the donkey,
she says, or the farmer's wife.

V

My boyfriend insists on picking me up from work
after the late shift. Streets that spawn jokes
during the daytime turn sinister in the dark.
No place for woman on a bicycle.
I remind myself to be patient. In two more months, everything
will freeze; snow and ice will trap everyone
indoors, making us all equals.

VI

The neighbor girl's father comes to the door wrapped in a parka
to warn us of recent break-ins on our block. He talks
about flood lights and a neighborhood watch, but
does not look my direction even once.
His true message
—*Son, guard close the things you love*—
is not for me.

VII

I remember one summer
back home in the California desert
when the rattlesnakes got so bad
the men all had to carry shotguns everywhere
they went. Or maybe there were no snakes
and they were just holding guns to hold
guns.

I Speak to You

Laurie Lamon

I speak to you, dragonfly,
twisting your neck as I look...

what matter,
what dust are you eating and eating?

Mother at the birdfeeder in a blue
day dress and slippers—

I speak to you across your field,
and at night through the window

whose curtains I cut and sewed
with young, terrible stitches.

I speak to you in your bed
when you reach for pills and water.

I speak to you from the chair
where I kneeled and sliced open

the ends of your slippers,
leaving my fingerprints on your ankles.

I drive slowly and look for the buck
who eats from your trees and beds in a dark

language of tiredness. I speak to you:
what death, what dust are we eating and eating?

All That's Said & Done

Laurie Lamon

The end of what was said
said nothing of itself said   *dome of sea*
is not of words   is done   & so the sea the sea
was no place was wilderness
unoccupied a swimmer on its back
one knee cast up   the end of what was said
resting & stroking

My Phone has 54 Missed Calls

Laurie Lamon

I leave it between bills, water/garbage,
ASPCA, or atop the ink-bled pamphlet
slipped beneath my door by the Jehovah's
Witness who comes in dark stockings,
a patent leather purse swinging at her elbow.

She wants me to know the end of the world
is coming here, to this front porch, where
hell is. But it's in the back where the neighbor's
voice screaming at his wife returns each
April, windows open—hatred and illness.
To the back of her coat, I say hell, yes.

What year is it? What time? How many voices
can memory hold like a dateline without
address, a trail of ants leading to catacombs?

Slow Moving Grain Train

Daniel Lee

The main intersection is blocked;
graffitied grain cars become the main aesthetic.
Passing in-between the cars
people chat on phones in automobiles—
ten frames a minute.
A train horn scores the soundtrack;
one conductor, nodding off
amongst flooded fields
while an audience of commuters
glare, as if in a television ad,
images but no words, except those
mismatched with lips.

American Daydream:

Skyscrapers, grain silos shed
concrete for glass;
the wheat grain falls,
mind stammering, grows
to a giant head,
golden sway, four hundred story
combine.

Minute turn of the wheels,
ten glimpses a minute,
slow train passes, this town,
halting
shrinking,
pondering art, dreams, grain.

Love Poem
Jane Brightwell Ligon

We smoked cigarettes and watched the stars, more stars than we had ever seen, and we lay on the cold winter road to look up. We already knew we were in love, the kind of love that slept and stirred and woke up screaming, it's face all fresh and bleary. It didn't matter then what loves had come before or what loves would come after, just that we'd known each other 13 days and this was the kind of love that we'd remember, the kind that happened all at once and burned like all the stars. We talked like we knew important things, like we were some great philosophers, and maybe we were, because how else could we love like this? How else could we fall without some fear that one day it would end? Maybe we had known each other years ago, before we (now) were born and the universe had somehow brought us back together, if the universe does things like that. We smoked cigarettes and watched the stars all spilled out in the sky, all burning years ago, their light not reaching us till now.

On the Centennial
of a Spokane Farmhouse
Paul Lindholdt

This scrabble of farm, carved from cloud,
coyotes and roosters launching loud,
in yodel and crow a century's home
comes to the future now to own.

Those who built the old barn wove
its loft and ladder, stoked its stove
and scraped until the basalt beds
gave way to house, a pond and sheds.

Hail Siegarts, Magers, Hampsons—those
who cracked the ice when the water froze.

Brooding Season
Paul Lindholdt

Further and further out the partridge flew
peeping, feigning a hurt wing, luring the dog
away from the hidden nest at field's edge,
landing on the weedy turf only long
enough to give the spaniel hope, open-mouthed,
bounding, oblivious to our commands.
We'd come in June, brooding season, eggs
still hatching, partridge chicks unfledged, wrong
to have brought our silky-coat trained
for the chase, lost in the knack to capture and kill.

If we were Puritans prone to morality tales
we might say a dog loses itself to instinct every day
while we lose ourselves only in the fall.
But we were living closely in the moment,
hooting for the partridge to escape and it did,
it duped the dog, this hunter we had bred to doze
at our feet. Our finest philosophies
may subtract no tension from the scene
or sketch it in ethical shades. From the field
we humans saw a partridge wing up and out of sight.

Along the Roosevelt Shoreline

Cara Lorello

Evening waits idle on the rocks, trading stories
with the surf of incoming tides.

Traces of sun welts worn raw move
sand crystals across imprinted stains
of blistering heat upon the last swimmer's back.

Stiff, sunned figures rise up from the sand, leaving imprints
surf waves wash away within seconds,
not a trace left behind.

A woman carefully wraps her child-like frame
in a cotton wrap pulled cold from inside a cooler
where all day it sat crumpled beneath crisp
orange skins and weeping beer bottles

so its fibers coat her reddened skin like aloe juices,
or the invisible hand pressing down
on the dome of the sun, spread like a pool of red
wax poured over an icy bath of deep blue horizon
as night touches down along the lake's border,
cool and silent.

Inhabitants trail back toward their parked vehicles
with soft, fluid steps, as if under water.

the ice attempts to explain itself
Seth Marlin

why i am the mountain and not the water—
this i am asked on occasions by the terns,
whom it turns out, in their high frantic tongue, have
no name for me. they speak of sun and of wind,
of sand and sawgrass, whales and damselflies,
even—yes—of man and of woman. but in their
endless keening, their great squalling councils,
they can never agree on how they should call me.
i cannot give them answer. i can only say that
the songs of things are flowing always, as i once
flowed. how it is only the leopard seals
who have some notion, basking black-eyed and
toothsome upon their floes. they call me implacable.
a term of relation. a term of reverence. how do i say
that what we aspire to is never the same as
what we are? in truth i could never be the ocean,
anymore than be a bird, or be a seal, or be a lover.

Past Ritzville

Tod Marshall

on the North side of I-90 near the first
exit, our pick-up sputtered, ran out of gas.
It was hot. You asked, "What is our status?
Where can we drink? What do we call a bird?"
I didn't know. We had few friends. Years later,
we remembered the beginning when a prince,
Nigerian and so rich, sent a desperate
email plea for help with big finances.
Back then, we never answered but someone
recently read it to a group of the living,
and we felt the pathos, wanted to give
him everything we'd ever had or known.

A Railing Is A Fence

Tod Marshall

A man threatens to jump. A bystander tries
to tackle him (the police cordon not quite
secure). He thrashes loose, climbs on the rail,
crouches and teeters, straightens his legs, waits,
and drops (a long second before the river
crushes his ribcage and he blacks out). Cold
water carries him downstream, smacks boulders
with his body, and finally delivers
him to a snag. His hooded sweatshirt loops
around a branch that bends but holds. On the bridge,
cops can't decide whether or not to charge
the hero: "I just wanted to save him."
Choppers circle. News crews hope for a scoop.
There is none, nothing, not even an image.

Carnivore
Tod Marshall

To roast, to scorch. To sear, blacken, or char.
To sizzle slowly beneath melting clouds
that drip into white clots of sun. We prepared
the meal with devotion and slow care.
Heat is a run-on sentence about the future.
Chew your meat, leave fat for a yellow jacket feast.

A Letter From the Time Traveler to Her Illustrated Man

Kelly Rae Mathews

My Dear Mr. Dark,

I know your carnival,
how it works,
how the gears and cogs
in your infernal machine
are electrified by suffering.

I know the ghosts by name who you've trapped in your mirrors
I know them intimately from when they were in bodies
and you, Mr. Dark, I know you, with your Dust Witch
and your corn-husk shape changing thrall
all, all your changelings in your carnival but you,
you didn't expect me here from all different kinds of time
all the stories we've known each other in
that I've illustrated on your body with my Cerulean Ink
and my Sharpest Pen and my Light, Bright, Quills.

So you're here, now again,
with the October People
in my town. I too, am of the fall,
but I'm the handle and the blade of the scythe
upon the wheat and corn
and I'm the hand that separates the wheat from the chaff
the hand that tills the earth
and digs deep the root cellar.

I am the cool and the shade, the shelter of a tree
after the over bearing heat of summer.

I am the one that calls
the weary traveler to rest on that fay hill to dream
by the lake, my eyes are wild
and I am she who is without mercy.
I am the one who loves the mystery of the Dark,
I am the one who knows the beauty of the Dark
and it is I who is the She that walks in that night.

And I'm here to tell you Mr. Dark,
with your spidery ways, and your many webs,
you are in for a surprise.
This is a city full of the Fall, and curses.
It's as haunted and desperate and disparate as its people.
And those with voracious appetites here do not take lightly
to outsiders eating their livestock without paying first,
but still, the city is alive, and I'm not giving up this ghost,
so I turn my nausea from repulsion into a belly laugh,
one convulsion into another,
just fast enough for me to avoid being stickied by you,
your arachnid strands, which attach like puppet strings.

I think I'm free. Then I find another invisible one.
Pull it out. Part of me goes with it.
The strands snap back to you or hang loose,
frayed, adrift, in need of sweeping.
Mr. Spider, Mr. Dark,
collector of all kinds of girls,
you fancy you like to fix us,
nice ones, mean ones, scary ones.
But we're not things.
And your first mistake was thinking I'm a girl.
I'm a woman.
Your second was thinking I needed fixing,
perhaps a putting in place, a clipping, here or there or
a dimming of my flamboyant feathers.

I like my wings,
thank you very much,
I don't want them clipped for your dark menagerie.
I'm not made of glass, but I'm not unbreakable.
I'm not the one who sings delicately for the emperor.
I'm the bird, who after I'm broken, I burn,
I live again in the ash, in the fire.

You've got the wrong bird,
Mr. Dark, I won't warn you by dying
if there's a problem with poison
in those mines you have in mind.

I'll make the Quills from my own wings,
and you'll say you're all surface
as I draw on you,
but those are just reflections.
I wanted to hear your introspections,
but I don't like being surrounded by mirrors,
and you have surrounded yourself with mirrors
and I have a tendency to drop mirrors.

So imagine what happens if you put me,
in your something wicked this way comes mirror maze.

All along you were looking for a new tattoo.
And this one my dear, is going deep,
where only you can see it
and by the pricking of my hot needle
I shall permanently illustrate upon your heart
what you shouldn't have forgot.
And that, Mr. Dark, is what you should have thought of
before offering me a ride on your carousel.

I'm not that kind of
Witch.

Mary

Brooke Matson

Her locus of control as misplaced,

the psychiatrist's notes said, as if she was a planet
that thought she was a moon.
Her hair had changed color
too many times so that it clung
to an ambiguous shade of strawberry.
Her step-father answered questions for her
too quickly and too often.
She had no body except
a whispered exasperation
around corners. Her grey eyes
floated on the stark landscape
of her face, a paleness unmarked
by lipstick or mascara, by color in general.

She was Mary, and no one noticed.

Burning Sage

Brooke Matson

You taught me to work yard sales, to browse
with an aloof air and point out damage
until they dropped the price

out of doubt. That was many years ago
before I moved away without explanation.
You must think I hate you, which is not

the truth. You scared me, that's all.
No doubt you burned sage
to rid your heart of splinters,

as you did for me once, when we burned
all the pictures I had of him
in your fireplace, even the ones

I loved. I wept a little,
watching the corners
curl into oblivion, and then

the pungent fragrance enveloped me.
You gave me the smoking bundle to hold.
Be free, you said, and I believed

I would be. Neither of us guessed
you also peeled from my skin
that very afternoon. You were the fear of love

that dissolved into a bold and bitter scent
that filled the room—so potent
we had to open the windows to breathe.

Every State Inside Her

Amy Silbernagel McCaffree

It smelled like old-growth Douglas fir
and Coeur d'Alene beach sand
surrounding his leave-no-trace national park,
just one state
away from Montana.
In the reflection of a quarter-moon
on a Tuesday, after reading Sherman Alexie
and eating sushi downtown.
It was quick, it was a Sunday—
dry and repetitive.
Lacked word choice,
sentence structure, love.
It was Hollywood, *Call you
tomorrow honey*, DJ funk,
Rock-the-Vote, *Happy Birthday*,
a Virgo-Libra
shake your bootie celebration.
Long distance *Holy Mary,
Mother of God* fantastic.

Target Practice
Stephanie McCauley

Thank god I tried archery at age ten
before the haystacks sprouted arms and prayed
for mercy. The thud of impact
felt like closure to me then, before I learned

a conclusion is merely a doorway
where some of us stop, backs turned
to the knob, slick grins on our faces.

But the haystacks sprout legs, too, even after
the millionth thud, and they tiptoe behind you
from Texas to Montana. When you grow suspicious
and turn back, they blend. You cannot catch

them at it. It's like looking for your feet
in the ocean.

Reveille
Adam McDaniel

Reveille rings commitments made
to answered national knocks yet revealed.
Run, roll, read, and rifle through red lands slain of soul.
Push, pull, pray and pain the soulless survivors.
Call answered.

[battle]

Voices leap from line to line overwhelmed by spread and bounds.
First letter smells of family pride.
Papered strength overcomes selfless and selfish walks on streets of brother-
    hood and country.
Scrolls roll themselves onto the deck like white, heavy-set clouds off Jekyll
    Island.
Warriors enveloped into the solitary longings of love and family, one week
    late.
Mail call.

Soldiering mellows in the night like Georgia corn whisky, leaving drunken
    hands covered in
grease leaked from lead and bolts.
Sleep again escapes the tired desires cast upon the cot.
He awakes with an abundant head in closeted inquisition of self, of enemy,
    and commands.
Complicit, delirium steers the tiller onto the field.
Reveille sounds Georgia Blues a mile from camp, "mamma can you hear your
    little boy calling
your name."
Call answered.

[battle]

Dear Gamma Ray Burst 140419A
Kristina McDonald

By the time you read this, you'll be dead.
A footprint of light in the sky, and then
nothing. It's like the discovery of anger
when you're five. Only a pinprick, and yet.
I ran over an animal last year, something small
and gray. I felt a jolt in my sternum
but when I looked in the mirror, it was gone.
I'm not afraid of dying, but I was afraid
to look in the coffin at my Aunt's funeral.
We dress our dead up like dolls and I
didn't even know her, would never know
the color of her eyes. I can only imagine
everything you've seen and swallowed
and left behind. Everything burns brighter
in the darkness and the truth is, I never noticed
you were there. Yesterday, an antelope
forgot her name. Yesterday, a clouded leopard
was born. 12 billion years ago, a star exploded
and yesterday I mourned you for the first time.
The truth is you've always been dead, but tonight
I can hold my hand up to the sky
and fit the shell of you between my fingers.
I can carry you with me like a piece of bone
the universe forgot to bury.

When the Mouth Gets Tired of a Diet of Dirt

Kristina McDonald

Outside, the old nowhere, the unreasonable theft
of a flower or silence as a form of desire.
Roots never go anywhere but down and maybe
it's rebellion, tendrils holding firm
but flicking off the world when no one's looking.

Because no one is really looking. Sailors never see
the carved woman at the front of their ship,
they make up her name and forget
her story. Meanwhile, she sleeps with her eyes open.
She sees everything but says nothing.

And isn't that how everyone likes it? The men
shit in buckets and the waves roll in and every day,
she drowns. If her lips could move, she would
politely cough. She would say, *I have something to say.*
And then, an ocean would spill out.

Following the Day

Dan Morris

I feel sad for him,
that dead German shepherd
on the right shoulder
next to a driveway
on 97, south of Okanogan.
Its people, gone, perhaps think
that he's happy,
running through orchards that wall in
their house, this road.
These trees fade to fields
of wheat cropped short
like a crew cut and yellow
as summer. I drove this road
to see where it went. A hamburger
in Wilbur, Vanilla Coke in Omak.
All in the rearview now
with that shepherd, apple trees, yellow
wheat. Grand Coulee, Spokane
miles away.
Over the speakers, Milo Aukerman
sings *everything's going to be okay*.

Watching an Eastbound Freight Train from my Northerly Window

Dan Morris

It's so late now the street signals
have turned to blinking. There isn't
time for wordy sentences. If leaves were
in the trees, they might have something

to say. I would surely listen.
The occasional car on I-90 slips past
this dying city like a yawn. All I have
is this window and the static of night.
Three engines and thirty-two
boxcars so far. The average
is one hundred. Will they stop
in Missoula or continue
on to Chicago? A moving mile
of metal drives me. I feel the clank
of wheel and track, the screaming
steel. It is more hopeful at this 3 AM
than waking at dawn.

The Cook Always Gets Her Way

Travis Laurence Naught

Grandma Dorothy has always made the best pies.
Mixing part ingredient, part hard work; her recipe
so simple. Make sure only the deserving take a bite,
or at least, those who taste a slice are surrounded
by knowing how much effort it takes to make flavor
compliment truly homemade meals. A roast raised
on family land, planted by hand, plowed each year
in a rotating fashion to keep from abusing pastures,
marbles evenly, melts in your mouth. Don't overeat,
dessert is your choice of peach, cherry, huckleberry,
with or without ice cream (à la mode never said, we
do not talk like that) please and thank you. Simple
phrases, polite conversation only around the table.
Her Eastern Washington farmhouse filled with men
who need gentle reminders after burning a day's
energy by 12 noon (the universal time for nipping
off the back porch bottle, whiskey, never spoken of
but taken with greater frequency later in the day)
before being ambushed by a pleasant, simple meal.

All bad language should remain with the animals
outside, in adjacent corrals after branding, cutting,
separating each calf from its mother, bull calves
from parts that never fail to elicit a ball joke or two,
to the chagrin of grandma. But she plays her part,
correcting immature verbiage in front of the youth
as a weekend teaching moment; cooked testicles
go by another name: Rocky Mountain oysters. She
makes sure her veiled threats reach the older men,
tries to keep her children's children innocent. Papa
alone was willing to try her. Love allows for testing
the limits and I once heard each of them wish death
upon the other with smiles on their faces, honesty

in their hearts. He explained it to me: hoping not to leave her alive, alone to deal with the pain burying a loved one brings. It all sounded very noble to me. But here's what I never understood until he passed (though I suppose I probably should have known), strong, able love is what makes grandma's pies best.

Breakup

Kurt Olson

The drunk hillbilly wasn't watching behind him:
that's why she ended up with a hook in her head.
Before I'd noticed, the skin had grown around the
barbs and she wanted me to just cut the line off.

"You gotta dig it out," I say as I approach,
knife ready, looking for muster and some earplugs.
And she cried and I cried and I yanked and I etched
a hole in her skin that bled for days but not weeks.

She wouldn't look at me while the tissue hardened.
Bathroom surgeons seldom see an "I owe you one."
But she twirled some fishing line hanging from my chest.
"I know," I said. "I'm a coward," and crawled away.

Driving Through Albany, OR

Margo Pecha

There's a McDonald's
down by the freeway onramp
where banged up kids slouch
on the concrete divider,
chewing dirty burgers
and pondering peeling soles
of sneakers in silence.

Where they watch cars
blur by in packs under
the harsh glare of
afternoon sun,
and wonder
what it's like
Out There.

In my dreams I blame you for everything

Kate Peterson

A nurse enters the room to hang a new bag of yellow fluid
and I stare out the window and realize I don't want to live
in a place without mountains anymore. My love for this town
made you hate it all the more when I left you. Yet somehow
you're still here. I'm sure you blame me for that.
The nurse leaves and my attention turns back to the child.
Steel is wedged in the basilic veins of both her hands
so I hold the pencil for her. We talk about spring.
I see strands of her long black hair floating, birds
making nests of it. She says when she cries
it sounds like ice, breaking and snapping apart.
I remember nights I came home from your apartment,
directly to the freezer to set icepacks on my eyes
so swollen from sobbing, I thought the lids might burst.
When I slept I dreamed you hit me, you were always so worried
that you might. We hear a helicopter landing and the girl says
she knows what it means. Some kid is dying in there.
There are so many sirens in this town. I should have warned you
that my earring would cut through the paper
and end up lost. That you couldn't fix it now
even if you tried. In my dreams I blame you
for everything—the air in your room
always spinning,
as if something so heavy
was about to touch down.

Braided

Kate Peterson

There is always something to be made of pain.
Louise Glück

The vacuum can't pull up the long thin fibers that have been floating around my apartment all week as I have been ripping and braiding and gluing to try to make something out of these days, to make a rug, something useful to step on. I carry the bag of fabric strips around with me, to a friend's porch where we sit and drink sour ale while the men who are interested in us now smoke thick cigars, and my friend decides she too will make a rug. We sit in our separate apartments, ripping and braiding, and because you and I still have most of our old friends, who see us separately now, quietly, you will see the makings one night on her floor, the long strands, the soft palette, and it will make me feel better somehow, to know that you know where she got the idea, and to know that you will picture me sitting alone on my floor with my back against the small black couch, aiming the orange glue gun, just trying to make something out of my pain.

Rubaiyat on a Summer Day

Jonathan Potter

We went to the bus stop, my daughters and I,
but the bus didn't come—we just looked at the sky.
We missed the damn bus, but that was okay,
we walked into Starbucks and drank—we were dry.

Then we hustled back out in the heat of the day
to catch the next bus that was headed our way.
We paid the buck-fifty, selected our seats,
sat back and enjoyed the roll and the sway.

We got off at the Plaza, where everyone meets,
and marveled at big cats, skywalked across streets.
Soon we were down where the river flows by,
searching for crawdads, blackberries, and treats.

The First Sign of Spring

Jonathan Potter

The short dark days of winter in Spokane
had been pulling at my pant legs
and sucking at my rubberized winter boots,

each day its own black hole suck
of frozen slush and muck,
when it's all you can do to get in the car

and drive to Safeway for a six-pack,
some baby food, bananas,
and Pop Tarts for tomorrow morning,

when what should my wondering eyes behold
but a fat girl doing a cartwheel
in the Safeway parking lot,

her buns like bowls full of jelly
in gray sweat pants, her tummy flesh
flashing out from under layers of winter clothes.

On Our Walk

Tim Pringle

You were quiet
and two steps ahead

so I watched how you
walked in your orange coat

and the river, green beside you—
the geese were silent

in the grass noticing you
as we passed

and as we crossed
the footbridge,

a man leaning on a bench
lit a cigarette over a book,

the willows carefully
dipped their boughs,

and the ducks made tiny
wakes through your reflection.

Slow of Tongue

Shann Ray

Middle-aged, we sat together
in North Spokane
on the hard wood chairs
of the state home
for the lost and spoke
of your sister's suicide,
her having fought
up a dark hill, clinging
to what life she had,
and I listened
like pale Moses, mute, unraveled,
trying hard not to look
so directly at the rage
burning in your eyes
like sorrow, like love.

In Spokane at the Montvale

Shann Ray

after Sonnet 116

We have come together to unwind
late evening when the world sleeps,
not only through grace and strength of mind
but in our loyal bodies dark and deep:
O Lord, we tremble. At the mark
of the arrow we come fully awake.
She grips my throat, opens the chart,
in the dark we declare what's at stake.

Not to resist the fall or the turn
of the evening, the bountiful run.
Not weft of wing or the hawk's cry
nor the tunneling roar of the engine.
  If we die tonight if the end comes
  we die together. Beloved. One.

Last Night Ferguson's Caught Fire

Laura Read

In the paper you can see the red booths
turned on their sides, their stuffing
leaking out. The fire spread next door

to the Milk Bottle, which is shaped like one
so you think of the bottles that clinked
on the porch in the first blue light

of morning, at the end of milkmen,
at the beginning of your life.
I went there once with a boy too sweet

for desire, after the Ferris Wheel
and The Octopus and trying not
to throw up on the grass and trying

to be sweet too, the kind of girl
you want to win a stuffed bear for,
one of the big ones that she'll have trouble

carrying, so you keep handing
the skinny man your dollars and his eyes
glint and you wonder what he's thinking

when he folds them in his pocket,
where he's going when he gets off,
not the Milk Bottle for scoops of vanilla

in small glass bowls. His heart is a book
of matches, his mind clear as the sky
in the morning when it's covered its stars

with light. In the winter, he'll hang
a ragged coat from his collarbone.
He'll think only of this year, this cup

of coffee, as he sits alone in his red booth.
If he walks along a bridge,
he might jump. And the river will feel

cold at first but then like kindness.
Last night a boy named Travis
killed himself

like young people sometimes do.
He told people he would do it.
They tried to stop him.

Now he'll have a full page in the yearbook,
his senior picture where he's wearing
his dark blue jeans and sweater vest,

leaned up against the trunk of a tree.
I wonder if he felt the bark
pressed against him

when he had to keep staring into the lens,
his cheeks taut from trying.
I wonder if he thought about the tree,

how could it keep standing there
without speaking,
storing all those years in its core.

People Don't Die of It Anymore

Laura Read

We're driving up Carnahan, winding south
towards the Palouse, its fields of wheat

at our periphery like hair.
This is the road where Robert Yates dumped

the bodies on his way home
to his five children, hearing the door

click open in their dreams
so later they'll say they knew.

My dad says the retirement home
we just passed, brick and lit with the cold

sunlight, used to be a sanitarium
for women with tuberculosis

and my sons ask, *What's tuberculosis?*
We're on our way back

from Greenbluff, constellation of farms
to the north where you go in the fall

for pumpkins and apples
and I can feel their beauty

in the trunk of the car, the thick fruit
beneath the ambrosia's skins, the seeds

we'll have to scrape out of the pumpkins
with a metal spoon and the strings

that will get under our fingernails
and hurt for days. St. Theresa

of the Little Flower died of it.
She was so kind in her biography,

always opening the door
for the gardener. And then she started

coughing blood and I mourned her
in my plaid uniform

and my Peter pan collar.
People don't die of it anymore, I say,

and we fall quiet for a moment and stare
at the houses on Carnahan,

their fences and dark windows,
their scribbles of smoke.

Blue Spark

Joshua Robbins

Back deck, Adirondack: evening hums.
Fly-by-nights kamikaze iridescence
into the zapper's electric blue.

Due west and past the river,
thunderclouds horizon summer's
thirsty ridgeline and I, moth

to fluorescence, stalk the moon.
Once, in a bar's back booth,
I was flesh jolted AC.

In the dance floor's strobe,
I radiated Plato, the Whitmanesque,
flashed the poetry of drag

and chrome, glittered vinyl, tiger print.
Outside, the city's turbines
churned the river's darkness white.

Now, summer rain
on oil-stained driveways, backed-up gutters,
the low river's drift.

Lightning spikes. I inhale the night:
lawn mist. Insect char. Beyond
the clouds, the electric moon.

This is a True Story

Mokeph Rusca

Carl the Canadian goose saw the water below
dotted with floating bodies.
They weren't dead, at least,
not yet.
They simply floated the river,
like driftwood,
radiating in the sun.
Carl watched them with growing curiosity.
They arrived in wave after wave of bodies...
only in the months when the sun is highest in the sky.
One area of the river in particular,
would cause the bodies to squawk and chatter excessively.
He soon realized that this area was special,
for the rocks were often visible close to the surface,
and the water roared more intensely.
The Geese People call this:
Shimmery Swift Noise.
With a staunch assertiveness
Carl the goose flew to the head of the rapids,
floated a portion of white capped waters,
then immediately swam to the nearest above-surface boulder
and stood on it.
Silent.
Motionless.
He
        had
                been
                        Rocked!

interstate death blues

Robert Salsbury

he said babe
we ain't playin possum
life happens at the exits
where the weeds blossom
the semis pull off
heat shimmerin off the cabs
all the drivers sleepin
their old ladies keepin tabs

she said hey dude
we ain't out of gas
punch them horses
burn the road real fast
fuck the bypasses
rest stops, gas stations
hitchhikers, bankers
the united nation on vacation

about then
a state trooper quakin on roids
blew past us like a lit fuse
an RV seen them escaped bat chain boys
in a dodge van
paneled with a stoned dragon
all hell broke loose on the interstate
30 some cruisers, couple paddy wagons

so he said
let's get some chow
there's a Howard Johnson's
comin up right about now

she said ok, man
let's get a room with a view
watch the sun set on the dregs of the day
he said cool baby real cool
a smoking room real close to the pool

Black Friday Night

Ryan Scariano

My jade plant start loves the logic
of streetlamps. She wants to prosper,
to grow under the moonlight.
She wants to shine off the gleam
in the snow. She feels what I feel
burning in the soft electric glow
from the Christmas lights
across the road. She wants to bloom.
For her, during even the darkest
hours, I will leave up the blinds.
She wants to sing her delicate white
stars through my steamy window and
out into the midnights of
a blessed and fortunate new year.

Father

Kaitlin Schmidt

Brown, gold-toe, wool. In your own house, you tuck together your father's socks and remember placing them in his big sock drawer when you were small. The dresser was as tall as the ceiling and housed hundreds of socks. They were longer than yours, they were grown-up length, all the way up his calves, professional, masculine, alien. You were scared and delighted to be so close to his smell. Maybe you wanted to climb into that drawer, but then he would find you.

When you were visiting your old home for Christmas one year, you didn't bring enough socks. He gave you a pair to borrow. When you left, you stole them. Now you are folding them in your own house, and you are taller than your dresser, and he is just a man.

Adam'ah

Michael Schmidt

In the dream my father's hands
are dark with soil. He takes my hands,
leans in close and cigarette breath,
tells me the grooves
are where dirt gets stuck, tells me
this is how people know
who you are. Then he is the earth
and my feet are big and I hate the earth

for having him,
for oozing from his head
instead of father-blood
when I found him on the ground
before I knew we could bleed:
Daddy's mudding, I said, unknowing,
like it was okay to lose everything
to the ground which does not cry out,
which has been an altar
all this time and the grooves
in my fingers are made
of trenches and graves.

Golden Rule

Kathryn Smith

This bridge spans a channel that cuts
the city in two. It's not the only way across, but it's the one
I've chosen, a path barricaded from the whip
of traffic and wide enough to pass a stranger

without brushing arms. Across the bridge, the Golden Rule
Brake Shop's readerboard announces this promise:
THE DEVIL'S BOOTS DON'T CREAK
Not until Sunday, anyway, when a man scales the roof
to rearrange the words into something
about a harbor and a ship. In the sub-freezing sky,

a solitary line of geese. They form no V,
no letters of use to the sign changer fighting the wind.
No help, either, from the abandoned phone books the next
doorway over, full of numbers, most of them
wrong. He'll have to find the message himself, find
the courage to stand so far above the city, steam
rising from its insistent river. The geese are long gone.
A SHIP IN HARBOR IS SAFE, BUT WHAT GOOD IS IT.

The City Council Welcomes the Christ Child

Kathryn Smith

Our city is near nature. It's near
perfect, our sidewalks pristine. We invite you
to take a seat and admire their beauty
if it's between midnight and 6 a.m.
But please don't linger and for heaven sake
don't lie down. If you're weary you can sit
at Starbucks for the price of a latte
as long as you don't take too long to drink it.
Are you just passing through? There's plenty of room
at the Lusso, the Dav, the new Worthy Tower.
Otherwise, keep passing. These restrooms
are for customers. This city is nothing
without its core. You must have somewhere to rest
besides the STA Plaza. Surely you see
that the planter outside the Olive Garden
is no place to lay your newborn. Why should we let
you loiter? What good can you possibly do?

Spokane is an America

Christopher Stuck

We're Wannabes and Has-Beens and Never-Couldas.
We're rich motherfuckers and poor bastards and really, no-kidding poor folk.
We're not the top. Shit, we're not even the middle,
but fuck you if you judge us for trying.

They say "Come to Seattle and you'll fit in wherever you want,"
but you belong here with the misfits.

They say "Go to Portland; that's a whole city of real misfits,"
but on your way home in your winter clothes,
Spokane will ask if you need something to eat
and be glad to hear you have some place to stay.
Because calling Spokane home might make you
look a bit homeless, and that's a whole new kind of being a misfit.

I know some other place is your capital-H, Home,
But Spokane might be your capital-O-M-E, hOME,
and no matter how high you climb,
Spokane will be waiting for you near the bottom,
a place for those that tend to roll downhill.

The Sound Came Out of the Woods

David Tagnani

I walked lightly down
a discarded dirt road
when I heard it come
across the meadow
from the stand of pine
The December sun, warm
on my face despite the chill
air, glistened the icy tips
of the blond grasses, each bowing
blade and lurking seed
white with light
But the sound
A moaning, low and desperate
from beyond the ponderosa
far past where the grass penetrates
at the forest's edge
before it succumbs to detritus,
duff, and darkness.
It is loud, pervasive,
singular, and sad
The breaking ice
on the lake yonder?
The song of a love-sick elk?
No, now is not the time
Now is the season of death

River Song

John Allen Taylor

Spokane rasps out the last breaths
of evening, and a man named river,
ice, stone walks heel to toe heel
to toe down Monroe St. Bridge singing
come down come down hearing
come down come down frantic like song
from the river, the ice, the stone below.

Spokane judders and creeks its way
into night—watches a man step
into light. Thinks not death, mobility;
not flesh, slag from the furnaces
of Hillyard, ghost of fire and sulfur,
city of dust and grain. The river sings
come down come down.

A man floats through Peaceful Valley
to West Central. Chaff that sinks like stone.
Is ice. Is river, now:
whatever he wasn't, whatever he once wanted,
furnace man, dust and grain; the river
sings and sings.

Sitting on a Wooden Bench by my Grandmother's Garden in Colbert, Washington

John Allen Taylor

remembering James Wright

A tree frog sits in my hand, heavy,
like three cold pennies, and shifts
back and forth on soft feet.
Across the gravel road, a buck and two does
pull at the bitter knapweed and eye
my grandmother's roses—
they will wait until I pluck a few hips for tea
and go inside for the evening.
Behind them, a yellow tamarack reaches toward
an early moon, shouldering a hawk's nest.
I lean back, feel the night settle on my forearms,
wait for the chicken hawk to come home.

Dear Spokane

Virginia Thomas

Spokane, I am curled tight in your fist,
exhausted
from chasing my own taillights
down your one-way streets.
Ten months since dragging
my belongings here, toward the rising sun.
Dark beer slides down easier now,
the light is harsher here but welcome, still.

You smell of lilacs and cottonwood,
you smell of concrete and urine.
Your art is dirty, your paint is new,
your motto is lightning, is blood, is clouds of vapor,
e-cig fake smoke floating over a haze of weary-eyed men
and gleaming young women.

You are a princess of an inland empire;
where, then, are your gems?
At the bottom of your swift, polluted river?
In the darkened wings of a downtown stage?
Under the cool blue glow of a burrito joint
crowded with bodies, lungs sucking in the ache
of the heart?

You hide from me, lilac city,
city of the children of the sun,
city of learning,
of metal and ink and timber.
Your alleys hear me, but
your streets don't recognize my soles.
Every step rhymes with a word you don't know,
a faraway something that doesn't jive

with Washington, where everything is washed,
continually bathed in revising and do-overs.

I know that much, Spokane, Spocompton, Spokanistan,
it is spoken, spat, splashed across every doorframe,
scrawled on street signs, sprawled over your bridges:
you don't give yourself easily,
but you are a place for second chances.

I remain semi-alien.
I press my ear to your curbs,
hoping to receive a signal in code.
Even your corners don't forget their beggars.
Even your parking lots echo with the humming voice of hope.
Just let me write my name somewhere small,
on a piece of you that bears no shame.
I'll be gone by the time you realize
I was ever here at all.

How it Went Down (King Cake)

Nance Van Winckel

It had her name written
all over it. She doesn't cut
the cake. She just digs
in. Every tooth
tearing through
a rainbow frosting
& angel white.

Chewing fast, nearing
the center & so
ravenous, suddenly
she's swallowed
the prize—the baby!—
bent as it was
in a fetal crouch.

That's how it went
down, & months later,
how it exits: bent &
wailing, having acquired
its own guts deep
at the sweet center
of insatiable hunger.

Burgeoning Snow Clouds

Nance Van Winckel

Reading your poems
starts the snow flurries that,
by page 46, become the blizzard,
which by sundown has closed the book of us

with all the marginalia I became:
little inky-eyed soul going fast into the gone
under ivory sheets and a back flap that bears your face,
old dear, holding me still.

Superior Experts

Nance Van Winckel

are due any
second to tell us
what X means, if
the blood left
on the street is cause
for such alarm
as this. The arc lights
striate us, one to
another. Were these not
our very own slums
once? Didn't we love
in spite?

Song of Spokane

Jess Walter

Our voices cried (*We will...*)
northside to South Hill
Wandermere, Qualchan and Manito
(*We will only...*) from Luna to Rancho Chico
and while test-driving a high-miles Chrysler
at the East Sprague Cheap Wheels
(*We will only be...*) sipping tea
at the service desk of Liberty Lake Mercedes
(*We will only be happy...*) at 24-hour Fitness
open all night for when the paradox hits us
that for all our talk of sustainability
the only way to avoid obesity
is to work off all these calories
on treadmills with our own private TVs.

(*We will only be happy when...*)
we confide to therapists in clinics and HMOs
We will only be happy when we get a Trader Joe's.
(They have them in, Seattle, you know.)

And on the day that ours opened
the therapists' eyes were bleary
from nights without sleep
as they made appointments to see
their own listless shrinks
and confess their deep-seated fear
that a whole city's sadness might disappear
when the lights came on at the Joe's here
It would be awful, the frightened therapists agreed,
if a new grocery store actually made us all...happy.

But not to worry.

No-one ever went broke in America—
in the unhappiness business...

And so even two-buck chuck
isn't nearly enough
to relieve the stuff
that collects on our dissatisfied parietal lobes
like January snow
I remember one from a few years ago
that caused all the streets to close
and the schools to shut down
and the sudden realization that perhaps in a town
of two hundred thousand
we might want to invest
...in a second plow.

But what I really remember
is my son and I building a snow fort
and having the county assess it
as worth more than our home
and how nice it all was
how peaceful and quiet
we couldn't even leave home
if we'd wanted to try it
let alone go for a chub of smoked gouda at Trader Joe's
which, flash to the day that it opened
was filled with those sleepless red-eyed therapists
thinking (*Now we will....*)
as they looked at their own shopping lists
—pasta, potstickers and a dry Gewurztraminer—
and as the real poet said, "Let be be finale of seem"...er

Maybe not.
Maybe the answer does lie
in a hand-crafted beer
And an apple-pecan pie
Which is why we ply those aisles with hunger and fear
as the voices cry (*Now we will...*) and you can hear

them pleading, from Ferris to Mead, LC to CV
(*Now we will only be...*)
flooding this river valley with our restless moods
Now we will only be happy when we get a Whole Foods.

And maybe it's not so crazy to imagine
salvation's pathway so fine and narrow
that they only sell it at Crate and Barrel
or that true joy awaits and fulfillment arrives
in aisles of organic beets and endives
(and honestly I don't even know what an endive is
or how to pronounce it
but I thought it sounded like arrive
and I see them on menus sometimes
but maybe I'm working too hard here to rhyme)
which reminds me that what I drive
is not my wife's Toyota Prius
but a 1963 Continental by Lincoln
in that most American of hues
the orange of prison jump suits
six thousand pounds of steel uni-body engineering
that gets nine miles to the gallon of premium
and I often feel the disapproval
of enviro-lefties like yours truly
thinking, *Don't you care about the world that you leave behind?*

You know.

For the children?

And that's when I have to force myself to recall
just how crappy other people's children are
like this little shit who sat next to me
on a three hour flight from Denver to eternity
this crazy lap child who kicked and fussed
and thrashed about wildly while his poor mom hushed
him and the rest of us recalled that movie
about the plane crash in the Andes

as the Mom gave Damien a Red Bull and some candy
and we wondered if a forty-minute delay was enough justification
to become cannibals—because there'd be no hesitation
about who to eat first...and that's when
Damien's mom smiled at me and said, *He usually travels so easily*
and with that Damien's head spun 360 degrees
and he delivered a roundhouse kick to my teeth
as flames shot out of his little shit eyes
and the mom said, *Honey, what's the matter with you tonight?*
and this monster kid looked up at me
and like some genius existential prodigy
in the voice of all humanity, he said: *I'm! Not! Happy!*

And us? What about us?
Will we ever be happy? I have no idea—
but I suspect that one day we will
when we finally get an Ikea.

It starts with a whistle,
and ends with a bark

Ellen Welcker

I was just talking about this with the Nebraskans.
I've had it up to here, they said, and pointed
at their necks and then I stopped listening; their necks
looked as though they'd been through a lot

40% of Americans think the devil is a person, that he
(or she) used to be a communist, but now he (or she)
is probably a terrorist. Their necks with the prickly heat,
with the sunburn, with the skin so sensitive to chafing

I've worked quite hard; I've earned this lapel pin. See how
a quality craftsman fence creates a beautiful
illusion of privacy? I'm proud of my card, look
how it portrays a mountain top as the pinnacle

of the human spirit. *Of course* the successful ego is lonely.
I am half Nebraskan, and it makes me feel good to dress up
my bare neck, now bejeweled, now bedecked
(so like a fleshy cephalopod cowering beneath the head)

I am a member of the Urban Lightwing Professionals and I
never leave home without my detachable bosom.
I've watched a rash devour a paint to tail and skullbones, oh—
a devil is a thing to pity, all inbred and cancer-faced.

Instant Replay :: Basal Ganglia like Exploratory Bump :: _____

Ellen Welcker

I keep thinking of the saltwater croc
how it gives the hypothetical
great white an exploratory

bump. The battle, inevitable,
as evidenced by both digitalized
& steel replicas of jaws crushing

watermelons. The way a great white
will barrel roll, even with a bitten-
off fin—a fin unlike a wedge

of watermelon. After the oceans
dried up they would be the last
living creatures on earth; not the

swans, like everyone thought, not
the watermelons or the saltwater croc.
Not the two-ton, million year-old

shark, no—camped among reef skeletons &
milling along the sandy ridges of the plastic-
laced ocean floor—I can hardly

say it: instant replay is to basal ganglia like
exploratory bump is to act of aggression. Like
when you said *human*, I heard *you man*, meaning

me: I am a member of the Urban Lightwing
Professionals, and I do not bend the rules.

Space Travel

John Whalen

Name is Mud.
Family name Mud. Town name Mud.
I've got callused hands, weird mind.

There is a thickness to the air in this town,
men hiding behind buildings,
someone riding a blue bicycle in the rain.

Fog's for breakfast,
anesthesia all afternoon, TV for dinner.
Tonight they're launching spaceships.

There are close-ups of the sky!
Oh, "space travel" is a pretty saying,
like "summer" or "pre-approved."

Next door is a moose painted pink.
Lawn forms and a radar dish in every yard.
Name is Mud and, yes, it's a pretty saying,

"s p a c e t r a v e l,"
one that does not mire itself on a furry tongue.
They are shining, slippery words,

far apart, yet personal,
as if Mud could escape town
running, leaping on his padded and thorough hands

across moonlit blacktop, through exhausted
suburbs and shopping plazas,
through the dangerous highway verbs and the nouns of leaving.

Space travel, space travel! Damn!
Mud's life is super-glued to a truncated Volkswagen van
hauling a swimming pool across town,

and my times are not those of an American hero.
But space travel! I'm talking about far away and lean
and sitting cool and fooling around with telescopes!

Yes, if just once Mud could step far enough away
to look back at the earth reflecting the sun
like a flipped coin, smooth and heartening as a nickel.

New Caledonia
John Whalen

Unfulfilled radicals working the phones
at a Communard call center at Hatch

and Pacific, Les Zutistes are talking,
talking. They are wearing skinny silk ties.

Their desks border pallets of tuna fish
that replaced brick walls. A day-one trainee

with last night's hashish pincering his skull,
Rimbaud stares at the guy demonstrating

head sets. "Talk into it like this. Easy."
At shift change, a set of rails with rollers

shuttles in cases of beer from the street.
Les Zutistes are firing up Marlboros.

The Single Celled Parameciums tune
their guitars. Rimbaud's got the microphone.

Whatever Newly Complicates Us

John Whalen

Portrait painter, fire fighter, reluctant witch.
I claim no more than the briefest
of occupations. No dairy farm
and nothing you've ever learned by heart.
Forest fire or not,
wind pushes chaff through the house
when no one's home to pay attention to me.
When I run, when I dive into caves
of tractor noise, when I kiss you,
that's all I'm doing: as if arranging
furrows in a field along these August hills.
Falling into flames, smoke jumpers sing:
fire on the mountain.
Whatever's new. Whatever's burning.

Walking Home, the Poet Treads Wet Maple Leaves

Caitlin Wheeler

Why do these ruddy
leaves, like glass in the gutter,
recall Thailand, that
bicycle ride, that man who
followed me home in the rain?

My Cat Says Goodbye

Caitlin Wheeler

"How should I say what it meant?"
I ask her.
She gets up, pushes her head
into my palm twice,
circles back to close her eyes and sleep.

Daybreak, Spokane, September 2001

Joe Wilkins

They're tearing down the Olympia Beer sign
from atop the Empire Hotel.

The geese wing south again,

above the char color of the city,
through the still dark house of the sky.

Last week a woman threw herself in the river.

       *   *   *

I dream winter—wind leaning hard
down the mountains, blown snow

and ice—reading James Wright
for the first time.

How sad and lovely,

because in his poems everything and everyone
was always dying,

yet looking up from the page
I had never before wanted so wholly to live.

       *   *   *

Across the black river, I watch

bricks fall from the hotel without sound,
flowers of smoke blossom above the coal stacks,
and now the first sun break shivers me
in my dew-soaked shoes.

It is time to grieve, to believe in the world again.

William T. Phillips

Joe Wilkins

*"[The theory is] that Butch Cassidy did not die in a shootout in
Bolivia in 1908, but assumed a new name, William T. Phillips, and
lived a quiet life in Spokane until his death in 1937. [...] A long,
rambling manuscript written by the elderly Phillips entitled The
Bandit Invincible [...] purports to be a biography of Cassidy. [...]
The manuscript also lapses, briefly, into the first-person."*
Jim Kershner, Inland Northwest History blog

At noon, he combs his mustache and puts on his bowler hat and walks down
the littered avenue to the lunch counter on the corner. It's noisy, the tables
filthy. The woman brings him meatloaf, always meatloaf, because he pays with
stories. He used to sell dictionaries door to door, but now his old bones clack
like dominoes in a cedar box and he can no longer bear the weight of all those
words. So, it's a good thing he doesn't mind meatloaf, it's a good thing the
waitress here is lonely too and loves his stories. He tries to be very careful.
He will say things like, *When he rode up the canyon, the night was big and
dark and far to the stars.* He will say, *Butch loved dogs. He had a yellow dog
named Sunday he loved very much. He almost didn't leave the country when
they wouldn't allow Sunday on the ocean liner. Near the end of his life, Butch
pined mostly for that old dog.* And later, after the woman has brought him a
second cup of coffee and he has thanked her and tipped his once fine hat and
she has smiled and shuffled away, he walks down the hill to the river. There
is a park there where most days he sits for a bit and thinks. Sometimes a stray
will come sniffing out of the willows and he will call to it. He loves dogs. He
knows that much for sure. Yet in the evening, the sun dying over the pines,
the mountains going blue and dark, he waits for stars that never look right, he
says to himself the names—*Old Bert, Kid Curry, Sundance, Sundance, Sundance*—that sound so exquisite and wrong. The street he lives on is paved. He
sleeps above a watchmaker's shop, all those tiny gears and bells. He is nearly
seventy years old in this city of coal smoke and automobiles. What did he do
to deserve this? What did he do? What did he do? He doesn't know. He walks
back to his room. He gets out a piece of rolled tin and a sheet of paper, loads

his old pearl-handled Colt and sets it on his desk. Now he dips the bent point of the tin into a bowl of blue ink and writes: *Butch knew he'd lived a good life. He was kind to women. He always had a shiny new jackknife for a boy. And that day, the sun bearing down, the dust of the road thick in the dry air, the whole Bolivian Army waiting outside, he wasn't scared. Six-guns blazing, I stepped out to meet them.*

Banish the Children

Tana Young

Use your hands to shape the soil
into ovals and rectangles,
neat, tidy and symmetrical.

Believe in hemlock, bitter-
sweet, yew, snake-berry, bits
of colored glass and nightshade.

Press them into mud, spread
over plywood and rusty nails.
If you're filthy when called

they won't mind you've gone
missing, that your body turns up
only then. Cruelties lack

color, especially.
The refurbished past
holds weight—a fulcrum.

Ritual-to-Ritual, dust-to-dust,
the pendulum swings, hands
on a clock. Banish this one, reinstate that.

Until, one day, we'll all wander away
and refuse to come when called.

Our Daughter's City

Maya Jewell Zeller

It is March. In the snowmelt,
when you walk the cliffs,
you can still see the metal needles
threading the sand, their tips
dulled to rust. Soon the dwarf
mountain lupines will drag
out their curtains of purple
to cover them, their shaggy blooms
raking, too, over condoms
at the periphery of the neighborhood
park, just beyond the slide,
its long yellow neck.
This is where our daughter plays. She
is old enough now to say *choo choo*,
point to train-scabbed valleys,
name the colors of trees, cars, a day moon
she knows by its curl of white.
She will know basalt by touch,
the butterscotch bark of pines. Soon I will show
her those fields where the cats ramble
like seeds, concrete gives way to a meadow.
She does not remember the summer we came
to Spokane. Feral cats roamed the empty lots
north of Target. The newspaper
showed two kittens stalking
a cricket, a calico glaring at the camera,
gold grass splitting her gaze.
The caption said they were multiplying
too fast for the city to spay them all.
The July horizon dulled to a haze less blue
than your eyes and stars
appeared across the night like stitches

trying to hold shut the sky even as airplanes
cut it open again.
We lay on our backs in the yard
and listened to the rip
of engines, watched the spine of lights arc
west toward Geiger field.
I wasn't yet used to heat
so you soaked washcloths in ice
water, laid them on my thighs.

Monroe Street: Route 24

Maya Jewell Zeller

The moon gets on a bus,
dragging her large bag behind her,
its amorphous, sexually ambiguous shape,
plastic bulging or pierced through
by triangles of green, silver
pond shards, swords and daggers
which cannot quite rip it. It's a Glad
flex bag, after all, and the bus
is a Greyhound, bound for somewhere darker
than she's lived before. She's leaving him—
the man who's beaten her
until she's grown thin as a fingernail.
We all know this story. There might be bare
feet, a bird on a branch which reminds the woman
she should be plucking feathers or grooming
her children. There might be a river, soda cans
with labels you can't quite read. There is caffeine,
grocery sacks. There is a huge shape bigger than anything
it follows. Jung calls it The Shadow,
and we call it our step-sister, or our college
lover, the snail that comes back to the cabbage
or the cat that lies curled every Saturday
at our doorstep, come in from the gray,
a crescent cut across her neck. It takes
a warm washcloth, twenty minutes of care
on linoleum. We wipe the blood
from the tub's corner. Outside, the rain
keeps coming, and we wrap the cat in a towel,
bring her around to neighbors to ask
whose she is. Each door opens to more
and more women smoking cigarettes.
The muted thump of guitar

in the background. In our arms
she lets out her sharp cry, mournful
and lunar, and we see now, when we turn toward
the street, a girl steps off the bus, white hair glowing,
and trailing her like a tired child,
the long black bag.
We're not sure if we can help her,
whether to look away
or approach,
and if we did,
even what we should say.

Contributors

Anastasia Aguon is currently learning how to be brave. Her words can be found on Spokane bridges, littered on coffee shop floors, and in hugs. She is studying theatre at EWU, while pretending she is omnipresent and can go on endless coffee 'meetings.' She drinks coffee. She'll probably like you. She is a poet, which means she will fall in love with you at least once. Tell her your story.

Zan Agzigian, a poet, story writer, and playwright, has devoted many years to arts advocacy and organizing in the NW. Her first collection of poetry, *Stamen and Whirlwind*, was published by Gribble Press in 2008. Zan collaborates with Bitterroot Salish poet Victor A. Charlo, co-writing contemporary Native American plays. She received her MFA in Fiction from EWU and lives in Spokane with her wonder dog, Itsy, where she is Community Producer of Spokane Public Radio's long-standing weekly eclectic program, *Soundspace*. "Carrying a Canvas, Midnight: Downtown Spokane" originally published in *Stamen and Whirlwind*, edited by Dennis Held, and published by Gribble Press, Spokane, 2008.

Mark L. Anderson lives in Spokane. He is a co-founder of the Broken Mic readings at Neato Burrito. He is a really interesting person who has never bored anyone to death.

Liv Larson Andrews is the pastor of Salem Lutheran Church in Spokane's West Central neighborhood. She lives with her husband, Casey, and their young son, Arlo. She dreams of hosting the first lectionary based cooking show.

Rumor has it that **Derek Annis** can be seen around Spokane moving piles of dust from one location to another, in a desperate and futile search for purpose. On cold days he wears heavier clothing than he would on warm days. He spends some of his time sitting in a chair, and some of his time not sitting in a chair. He is already dead, and is survived by a violent writhing mass of meaningless nothing. His poetry has appeared or is forthcoming.

Jacquelyn Barnes is a freelance copyeditor, writer, and designer—as well as a barista at Indaba coffee bar (because she loves West Central and needs a reason to get out of the house on a daily basis). She has a Bachelor's degree in English from Whitworth University. Although originally from Portland, she has elected to stay in Spokane and currently lives on Mallon Avenue in West Central with her newly wedded husband Ty.

A 2014 Washington Artist Trust Fellowship recipient, **Polly Buckingham** was a finalist for the Flannery O'Connor Award in 2011, 2012, and 2013. Her chapbook, *A Year of Silence*, won the Jeanne Leiby Memorial Chapbook Award for Fiction and was published by The Florida Review Press. Her stories and poems appear in *The Threepenny Review* (reprinted on *PoetryDaily.com*), *The New Orleans Review*, *The North American Review*, and elsewhere. She is founding editor of StringTown Press and teaches creative writing and literature at EWU. "The River People" and "The Last Day of January" first appeared on *cascadiareview.org*, January 2013.

Libby Burnette is a recent graduate of the Inland Northwest Center for Writers, Eastern Washington University's Creative Writing MFA program. She writes fiction and poetry and is currently working on a collection of short stories.

D.S. Butterworth teaches literature and creative writing at Gonzaga University. His poetry and fiction have appeared in many magazines and journals. Algonquin Books published his creative nonfiction book, *Waiting for Rain: A Farmer's Story*. His two volumes of poetry published by Lost Horse Press are *The Radium Watch Dial Painters*, which was a finalist for the Washington State Book Awards, and *The Clouds of Lucca*.

Since October 2013, **Thom Caraway** has served as Spokane's poet laureate. In that time he has given many readings, and is grateful for those opportunities. He has also tried to get more of Spokane thinking about literature and creative writing in Spokane as a broad, multi-faceted community filled with diverse interests, so that pockets of activity are in dialogue and commerce with each other. He hopes he has been successful in some small way. He lives in the West Central neighborhood with his wife, children, housemates, pets, and many chickens.

Aimee R. Cervenka holds a BA in Biology from Rollins College in Winter Park, Florida, and an MFA in Creative Writing from EWU, where she currently works for the TRIO Student Support Services Program as a retention specialist. Her work has appeared in *Poet Lore* and *The Ampersand Review*. "Spill" was previously published in the Fall/Winter 2012 issue of *Poet Lore*.

Rebecca Chadwell was born and raised in Spokane, along with her cousins, brothers, sister, ducks, and feral rabbits. She enjoys writing for print and film, as well as working in sound design and art installation. When choosing which conversation killer to use in out-of-town collaborations, "I am from Spokane" always wins over "I am from Washington. State. Not Seattle."

Matt Comi lives, writes, and gardens in Spokane. He likes parsnips. His poetry, essays, and interviews can be found in *Sugarhouse Review*, *Weave*, *Nat Brut*, *Birkensnake*, and *Rock & Sling*.

Spokane poet **Chris Cook** is author of *The View from the Broken Mic*, published by Gray Dog Press. His writings are also contained in *Spokane Shorties*. Additional poetry has been published by Meadowbrook Press, *Scholastic*, and *The Spokesman-Review*. He is the winner of the Terrain 5 All-Star Poetry Slam, the 50-Hour Poetry Slam, numerous *Spokesman-Review* Limerick contests, and the Naked Lunch Break Limerick Slam. Chris is the current Grand Slam Champion for Spokane Poetry Slam, for which he'll be representing Spokane at the 2014 Individual World Poetry Slam. He has competed in 2 National Poetry Slams. Chris is the organizer and host of "3 Minute Mic," Auntie's Bookstore's monthly open mic poetry event.

Beth Cooley has published poetry, essays and fiction, including two novels with Delacorte Press. Her work has appeared in *Willow Springs*, *Mid-American Review*, *Poet Lore*, *RiverLit*, *Rock & Sling*, *Wisconsin Review*, and other journals. She teaches literature and writing at Gonzaga University and lives in Spokane. "Manito" originally appeared in *Roanoke Review*.

Brian Cooney grew up in New York, picked up a PhD from University of South Carolina, and lives now in Spokane, where he teaches literature at Gonzaga University. His poems have appeared in or are forthcoming from journals including *Eunoia Review*, *New York Dreaming*, *The Bicycle Review*, *Pacifica Literary Review*, *Crack the Spine*, and *Floating Bridge Review*, who awarded him the 2014 Paula Jones Gardiner Award. His chapbook *The Descent of Ham* will be published by Alice Blue in 2015. "On the Universal Tendency to Debasement in the Sphere of Love" was previously published in *Crack the Spine* Issue 117.

Linda Cooper lives in Seattle, where she teaches middle school Language Arts. She completed her MFA at Eastern Washington University, and she misses Spokane's laidback and unpretentious atmosphere. Her poems have been published in *Hayden's Ferry Review*, *West Branch*, *Many Mountains Moving*, *Willow Springs*, *Third Coast*, *Hubbub*, *Elixir*, *Diner*, *Midwest Quarterly Review*, and *Rock & Sling*.

Mikayla Davis is an undergraduate from Spokane. She has a BA in English from Eastern Washington University as well as several two-year degrees from Spokane Falls Community College. She is the editor for *The Wire Harp* and has poems published in *Northwest Boulevard*, *Gold Dust*, and *CandleLit*.

Tom I. Davis was born in the town of Milan on the Little Spokane River and lived in at least 24 communities within the state. He taught high school English, authored *The Little Spokane*, directed a play, and was the father of seven children.

Krista Marie DeBehnke is a doctoral student in English at the University of Louisiana at Lafayette. She also serves as the poetry editor for the online literary magazine, *Rougarou*. She is a recent graduate of Eastern Washington University's MFA program. Her poetry has appeared in *The Portland Review*, *Up The Staircase Quarterly*, and is forthcoming in *Rock & Sling*.

James Decay lives in Spokane, Washington. He is a full-time construction worker and a part-time poet. He began writing two and a half years ago during a stint in prison where he found self-expression through poetry. He hopes that sharing his stories will encourage others to do the same.

From his corner office at Gonzaga (shared space in an annex—but still, CORNER OFFICE), **Jeffrey G. Dodd** likes to irritate folks who take themselves too seriously. Especially Thom Caraway. That guy. Is he something else, or what?

Michelle Bonczek Evory is the author of *The Art of the Nipple* (Orange Monkey Publishing, 2013) and the forthcoming Open SUNY Textbook *Naming the Unameable: An Approach to Poetry for New Generations*. Her poetry is featured in the 2013 *Best New Poets* Anthology and has been published in over seventy journals and magazines, including *Crazyhorse, cream city review, Green Mountains Review, Orion Magazine*, and *The Progressive*. She holds a PhD from Western Michigan University and MFA from Eastern Washington University, taught most recently at SUNY College of Environmental Science and Forestry, and mentors poets at The Poet's Billow (thepoetsbillow.com). "The Hitchhiker" appeared in *Permafrost* and then in *Slipstream*.

Lauren Gilmore was born and raised in Spokane. Her poetry has appeared in *Riverlit* and *The Wire Harp*, and is forthcoming in *The Floating Bridge Review*. She was the 2013 Spokane Poetry Grand Slam champion and the recipient of the 2014 Richard Baldasty award for poetry. Her first full-length collection of poems *Outdancing the Universe* will be published by the University of Hell press in 2015. She also writes stories and love letters to insects.

Born and raised in Spokane, its familiar views and locations have always been comforting to **Lindsay Golden**. She graduated from North Central High School. She's lived off of Garland, on 7th, and in between. She's going into her sophomore year at Eastern Washington University to pursue a degree in Children's Studies and a career as a Child Life Specialist.

Isaac Grambo has been involved with slam poetry since 2006. He represented Boise, Idaho, at the National Poetry Slam four times between 2006 and 2010, and acted as Event Manager for slams in Boise for four years. He moved to Spokane and resurrected Spokane Poetry Slam in 2012, and has been its commissioner ever since. In 2013, Grambo was the Host City Coordinator for the Individual World Poetry Slam, held in Spokane. He taught in the Art and Communication departments at Boise State University for five years, and currently resides in Browne's Addition.

Michael Gray won a 2012 AWP Intro Journals Project Award and the 2013 Hot Street Emerging Writers Contest, was nominated for *Best New Poets 2014* and named a finalist in the 2013 Concrete Wolf Chapbook Competition and *The Lit Pub*'s 1st Annual Poetry Contest. Translations of Yau Ching appear in *Shadow Beings* (XXX Zines, 2014). Work appears or will appear in *Rock & Sling, Hot Street, Cha: An Asian Literary Journal, Poetry East West, Puerto del Sol, theNewerYork, Fence,* and elsewhere.

Timothy Greenup teaches writing and literature at Spokane Falls Community College. His poems have appeared in *Redivider, LEVELER, interrupture*, and elsewhere.

Tom Gribble is a poet, publisher, and teacher. He has an MFA from Eastern Washington University. He teaches English at Spokane Community College. Tom was awarded a fellowship from the Artist Trust, the AWP's Intro to Journals Project (poetry), and others. His work has appeared in *Sierra Nevada Review, Puerto Del Sol, Glass* and other fine journals. His current project is *The Fifth Trumpet.*

Iris Gribble-Neal has lived in Spokane for 40 years and in Eastern Washington for most of her life. She can breathe here, and her eyes have far horizons to see. The poems included here are about Spokane or Eastern Washington or people she has known here, lives on the line most days, bloodied by the scabbed land. With her husband, Tom Gribble, she has been both editor and publisher of Gribble Press and before that the poetry journal *Heliotrope*. Her poems have been published in various journals over the years, including *Pontoon* and *Cascade.*

Emily Gwinn is a graduate of Eastern Washington University's MFA program and teaches English at Spokane Falls Community College. Her chapbook *Transpiration* was published by Finishing Line Press and her work has been featured in *Rock & Sling, Pontoon,* and *Hubbub*. Gwinn is a past recipient of the Tom Pier Prize in Poetry and has work forthcoming in *Pontoon*. In August, she represented Spokane at the 2014 National Poetry Slam in Oakland, California.

Elizabeth Hansen is fifteen years old and lives in Cheney with her parents, sister, and one of her four brothers. She is currently a sophomore at Cheney High School, plays the flute, mellophone, and alto sax in the concert, marching and jazz bands, respectively. She enjoys photography books, and looks forward to debate club. She has been writing for as long as she can remember and plans on being a professional author after college.

Stine Hansen found Spokane by way of a blown engine on an '88 Westfalia. A recovering food worker, she now studies visual communication design. Her daily haiku practice started in May 2013, prompted by a mid-afternoon murder in her neighborhood. Previous work appeared on King County Metro Buses.

Dennis Held's poetry has appeared in the *Alaska Quarterly Review, Poetry*, and *Willow Springs*, and his essays and book reviews in *Poets & Writers, Terrain,* and *The Inlander*. He has published two books of poetry: *Betting on the Night* and *Ourself.* He lives in Vinegar Flats, along Latah Creek.

Kimiko Hirota is currently growing up in Spokane. Her writing has appeared in *RiverLit*. Most of the time you'll find her studying for school, smiling at strangers in the poetry community, or rushing to whatever is next.

Jackson Holbert is originally from Nine Mile Falls, Washington, and now studies English and Creative Writing at Brandeis University. His work has appeared or is forthcoming in *Tupelo Quarterly*, *Thrush Poetry Journal*, *A-Minor Magazine*, *Stone Highway Review*, and *Camroc Press Review*, among others. He reads for *The Adroit Journal*, *The Blueshift Journal* and Lost Horse Press's Idaho Prize for Poetry. "Fragments" originally appeared in *Tupelo Quarterly*.

Christopher Howell has published eight full-length collections of poems and has two more forthcoming, plus a collection of essays and an anthology. He has also been awarded two National Endowment Creative Writing fellowships, and fellowships from the Massachusetts Council on the Arts, the Oregon arts Commission, the King County Arts Commission and the Washington Artist Trust. He has also been awarded the Washington State Governor's Award, the Washington State Book Award, and a number of other prizes and distinctions. He founded Lynx House Press in the mid-'70s and was its director and principal editor for 30 years and has been the director and senior editor of Eastern Washington University Press, and editor of the journal *Willow Springs* and several other literary publications. "A Party on the Way to Rome" was published in *Poetry Northwest* (1999), *The Pushcart Prize XXIV* (The Pushcart Press, Wainscott, NY, 2000), *Light's Ladder* (University of Washington Press, Seattle, 2004), and in *Dreamless and Possible: Poems New and Selected* (University of Washington Press, Seattle, 2010). "First Touch" appeared in *The Gettysburg Review*, 2005), *Gaze* (Milkweed Editions, Minneapolis, MN, 2012)

Kristine Iredale deployed with the Washington State Army National Guard's 81st Brigade Heavy Combat Team in Operation Iraqi Freedom from August 2008 to August 2009. Currently, she is a senior at Eastern Washington University. Besides poetry Kristine loves flowers, traveling, tattoos, belly dancing, and the culinary arts.

Mischa Jakupcak is from Missoula, Montana. She received a BA from University of Arizona in Creative Writing & Philosophy and earned a MA in Filmmaking from the London Film School. After working in film production on over thirty features in the Northwest, she produced the critically acclaimed film *The Off Hours*, directed by Megan Griffiths, which premiered at The Sundance Film Festival. She and her husband, Robyn Miller, created Zoo Break Gun Club, which released the film *The Immortal Augustus Gladstone* last year. Her first short film, *The Hero Pose*, is currently screening at festivals worldwide. *The Inlander* published her short story "Cha Cha" last year. She's a co-director at the local non-profit arts organization INK Artspace and is working on several projects. She lives in Spokane with her family.

Jonathan Johnson has published two poetry books, *Mastodon, 80% Complete* and *In the Land We Imagined Ourselves* (both Carnegie Mellon University Press), and the memoir, *Hannah and the Mountain* (University of Nebraska Press). His poems have appeared in *Best American Poetry*, been read on NPR's *Writers Almanac*, and appeared recently or are forthcoming in *Ploughshares, Missouri Review, Witness, New Ohio Review*, and *Poetry Northwest*. He is the playwright of the full-length play *Ode* about John Keats and Fanny Brawne. Johnson migrates between Upper Michigan, Scotland, and Washington, where he is a professor in the MFA program at Eastern Washington University.

Aileen Keown Vaux graduated from Eastern Washington University's MFA program in 2013. Her poems and fiction have been featured in *Windy City Times*, Chicago's "RUI: Reading Under the Influence," and the *Vita.mn* Summer Story series. She currently teaches at Spokane Falls Community College.

Scott Kinder-Pyle is an adjunct professor at Gonzaga and Eastern Washington University. As a New Church Development pastor in the Presbyterian Church (USA), he became interested in the poetic dynamics of leadership, and recently pursued and received an MFA from the Inland Northwest Center for Writers. He lives in Spokane with his spouse, has two adult children and enjoys walking his dogs on the 'trail.'

Laurie Klein thanks generous mentors, editors and judges for ushering her poems into print. Prizes and publications include: The Thomas Merton Prize, Predator Press Chapbook Prize, and a San Juan Writer's Fellowship as well as poems in *Southern Review, New Letters, Ascent, MAR, Terrain, Commonweal*, and others. A co-founder of *Rock & Sling*, she applauds its vibrant resurgence in the Spokane community. "Thinking About John G. Lake's Grave" appeared in *The Pacific Northwest Inlander*.

Leyna Krow has an MFA in fiction from Eastern Washington University. Her short stories have appeared in *Prairie Schooner, Hayden's Ferry Review, Ninth Letter, South Dakota Review, Santa Monica Review*, and other publications. She lives in Spokane with her boyfriend, dog, and one house plant.

Laurie Lamon has lived in the Pacific Northwest and taught poetry workshops and literature seminars at Whitworth University since 1985 (where she is associate professor of English). She received her doctorate from the University of Utah and her MFA from the University of Montana. Her poems have appeared in many journals and magazines, including *The Atlantic Monthly, The New Republic, Ploughshares, Colorado Review, Arts & Letters Journal of Contemporary Culture, Primavera*, and *Poetry Northwest*. She is the recipient of a Washington State Artist Trust Award in 2005, a Graves Award in 2002, and a Pushcart Prize in 2001 for the poem "Pain Thinks of the Beautiful Table." She lives with her husband William Siems and their two Scottish Terriers, Maude and Li Po.

Daniel Lee was born in Spokane and lived the first 29 years of his life there. Some of his earliest memories of the city were watching freight trains with his father and brother. Daniel works as an English instructor and now lives in Seattle with his wife and dog.

Jane Brightwell Ligon lived in Spokane from the time she was 8 to the time she was 18. Spokane held her as she went through school, fell in love, fell out of love, and became an adult. Though she lives in Seattle now, attending UW for creative writing and graphic design, Spokane will always be home.

Paul Lindholdt, a native of Seattle, worked throughout college as a homebuilder, industrial waste technician, Teamster, and longshoreman. His writing has won awards from the Academy of American Poets and the Society of Professional Journalists. In 2012 his ecological memoir, *In Earshot of Water*, published by the University of Iowa Press, received the Washington State Book Award. He lives in Spokane with his wife and his two boys, and is Professor of English at Eastern Washington University. "Brooding Season" appeared in *Entanglements: Ecopoems*.

Vachel Lindsay, 1879-1931, was a widely acclaimed troubadour poet, who, for a time in the 1920s, called Spokane home, took up residence in the Davenport Hotel, and married a local woman with whom he had two children before moving back to his native Springfield, Illinois. The poem on the back cover of this volume was written during his time in Spokane, and was originally printed with the illustration that accompanies it. Both are used here by permission of his estate.

Cara Lorello is a native of Spokane and graduate of Eastern Washington University. Lorello published her first poem in 1994 at the age of 13. She worked a number of years as a journalist and magazine contributor before pursuing poetry and creative nonfiction writing. Lorello's poems have appeared in *The Sun, The Smoking Poet, SlushPile, RiverLit, The Dissident, Wire Harp* and *Wulfstan's Miscellany*. Her articles have also appeared in past issues of *Northwest Woman, Spokane-Coeur d'Alene Woman* and the now out-of-print *EVE* magazine.

Seth Marlin holds an MFA in Fiction from Eastern Washington University. His stories and poems have appeared, or are forthcoming, in *The Way North, Underground Voices, Knockout,* and *Silk Road Review,* among others. He is a 2014 Pushcart Prize nominee for poetry, and the author (under pseudonym) of the critically-acclaimed Iraq war blog *Calm Before The Sand.* He makes his home in the Browne's Addition neighborhood of Spokane, WA, with his wife and dog.

Tod Marshall lives in Peaceful Valley and teaches at Gonzaga University. He has a little dog named Teddy.

Kelly Rae Mathews is originally from San Diego and moved to Spokane in 2004. Her articles, poems, and short stories have appeared in *Fickle Muse, The Kolob Canyon Review, Falling Star Magazine, Acorn, The Coyote Express, The Outpost,* and *Southern Utah University News.* She completed an anthropological research project on poets of the Inland Northwest, interviewing over two dozen poets, their audiences, friends, family members, and local business community who supported the poetry performances. Mathews gave the presentation, "How Poets Build Community: Reclaiming Intimacy from the Modern World," at the Northwest Anthropological Conference, the Eastern Washington University Creative Symposium, the Eastern Washington University Women's Center and Naked Lunch Open Mic.

Brooke Matson is a poet and educator. She attended Gonzaga University where she received her B.A. in English and her M.A. in Educational Leadership. *The Moons,* her first full-length collection of poetry, was published by Blue Begonia Press in 2012. Her poetry has also been published in *Floating Bridge Review,* several anthologies, and various issues of *RiverLit,* for which she is currently the 2014 Poet in Residence.

Amy Silbernagel McCaffree is a freelance writer and mother of two young children. Mountains, forest trails, and waterways inspire both her poetry and her work as a senior writer for *Out There Monthly,* the Inland Northwest guide to outdoor adventure, travel, and the outdoor lifestyle. She has an MFA in Creative Writing (2005) from EWU's Inland Northwest Center for Writers.

Stephanie McCauley is an MFA candidate at Eastern Washington University. Her poetry has been featured in *Burningword, Torrid Literature,* and *Blue Monday Review.*

Adam McDaniel, originally from Alabama, is a member of the Washington Air National Guard and works as a political aide when not in uniform. He lives in Spokane with his dog Cleo.

Kristina McDonald received her MFA from Eastern Washington University, where she served as poetry editor of *Willow Springs.* She has worked for literary non-profit organizations Writers in the Schools and Get Lit! Programs. Her poetry has appeared in numerous journals including *Narrative, New Guard Review, Sugar House Review,* and *Yemassee.* Her chapbook *Stories I Tell My Godmother* is forthcoming from Dancing Girl Press.

Dan Morris teaches writing and literature at Auburn University. His chapbook, *Following the Day,* was published by Pudding House Publications in 2007. His work has appeared in *Connecticut Review, The Cape Rock, Poetry South, Rock & Sling,* and *Xavier Review,* among others. He is senior editor for the online poetry journal, *Town Creek Poetry.* "Following the Day" was originally published in the chapbook *Following the Day,* Pudding House Publications, 2007. "Watching and Eastbound Freight Train from my Northerly Window" appeared in *StringTown* 8, 2005, and then included in, *Following the Day.*

Travis Laurence Naught is a poet who happens to be a quadriplegic wheelchair user. Collections of his work have appeared in paperback form, *The Virgin Journals* (ASD Publishing, 2012), and in electronic format, *Still Journaling* (e-book, 2013). Eastern Washington University brought him to the Spokane area in 2001 where he completed a BA in psychology and graduate work in sport psychology. Poetry helps Travis keep the wheels turning every day.

Kurt Olson is a part-time writer and part-time shoe salesman who lives in Spokane. He believes the importance of writing does not exist within the writer but within the audience. He really loves Jack Gilbert and Vera Pavlova. His ideal night includes whiskey on the rocks and Bruce Springsteen's "Nebraska" on repeat.

Margo Pecha is a Spokane native with a BA in Creative writing from Eastern Washington University. She's currently pursuing her MS in Book Publishing at Portland State University, where she is a copy editor for *The Portland State Vanguard* and *Pathos* literary magazine. In her free time she enjoys walks with her corgi, Archie, and eating doughnuts.

Kate Peterson is a graduate of the MFA program at the Inland Northwest Center for Writers at Eastern Washington University. Her work can be found in *Apiary*, *Barnstorm*, *Glassworks*, and the *Eat This Poem* anthology. She is originally from New Jersey, but has made Spokane her home.

Jonathan Potter, the author of the poetry collection *House of Words* (Korrektiv Press, 2010), lives in Spokane with his wife and daughters. His poetry has recently appeared in *Dappled Things*, *RiverLit*, the *Imago Dei* anthology (Abilene Christian University Press, 2012), and on *The Writer's Almanac* radio show. His work has also appeared in the *Hotel Spokane*, *Only Time Will Tell*, and *Verbatim* collaborative gallery exhibits. Potter moderated the "Poets of the Pacific Northwest" panel at the Get Lit! 2014 literary festival, and for the past three winters has hosted Naked Lunch Break, a seasonal literary open mic and reading series at Eastern Washington University's Riverpoint Campus. "The First Sign of Spring" appeared in *House of Words*.

Tim Pringle is a recent graduate of Eastern Washington University's MFA program with a concentration in poetry. He misses Spokane's trains the most, as well as walks along the river, and feels ever indebted to the community's support and diverse artistic identity. Since graduating, he has retreated west to be nearer the sea. He currently resides in Newport, Oregon.

Shann Ray teaches leadership and forgiveness studies at Gonzaga University, and lives with his wife and three daughters in Spokane. Winner of the American Book Award, the High Plains Book Award, and the Bakeless Prize, he is the author of *American Masculine* and *Balefire*.

Laura Read has published poems in a variety of journals, most recently in *Silk Road Review* and *Alaska Quarterly Review*. Her chapbook, *The Chewbacca on Hollywood Boulevard Reminds Me of You*, was the 2010 winner of the Floating Bridge Chapbook Award, and her collection, *Instructions for My Mother's Funeral*, was the 2011 winner of the AWP Donald Hall Prize for Poetry and was published in 2012 by the University of Pittsburgh Press. She teaches English at Spokane Falls Community College and lives in Spokane with her husband, Brad, and their two sons, Benjamin and Matthew. Both "Last Night Ferguson's Caught Fire" and "People Don't Die of it Anymore" were originally published in *Willow Springs*.

Joshua Robbins is the author of *Praise Nothing* (University of Arkansas Press, 2013). His recognitions include the James Wright Poetry Award, the *New South* Prize, selection for the *Best New Poets* anthology, and a Walter E. Dakin Fellowship in poetry from the Sewanee Writers Conference. He is Assistant Professor of English and Creative Writing at University of the Incarnate Word. He lives in San Antonio. "Blue Spark" appeared in *Praise Nothing*. Copyright 2013 by The University of Arkansas Press. Reproduced with the permission of the University of Arkansas Press, www.uapress.com.

Though born and raised in Spokane, **Mokeph Rusca** is a cultured, worldly gal who changed her name from the given 'Jolene,' after wandering the globe for many years. Pronounced 'moe-KEY-fuh,' the name means Born of Fire and reflects her passion for Nature and the death/rebirth cycles. She is a full-time gardener and friend to all creatures. She hasn't been published since college, over 10 years ago; she is honored to be part of this anthology.

Robert Salsbury is a tried and true Spokanite, born and bred, who works during the day as a DSHS program administrator and writes when he must. He won the 2010 *The Inlander* short fiction contest with his cheerful story about juvenile justice in a dystopic hellscape. Bob loves both the wild ocean beaches of Olympic National Park and the desiccated basalt shrub-steppe of the rest of the state. He alpine skis, canoes into the wilderness, and paints with an airbrush. He is raising and adopting his four-year-old granddaughter, Sophia, who makes everything better.

Ryan Scariano was born in Missoula, raised in Portland, and is now at home in Spokane. His first chapbook, *Smithereens*, was published in 2013 by Imperfect Press. He's a second year student in the MFA program at Eastern where he teaches composition. For many of the years between undergrad and grad school Ryan drove a truck, delivering oxygen tanks and hospice equipment. He has an out of the way website at: ryanscariano.com. "Black Friday Night" was previously published online at radicaldivorce.com and at inknode.com.

Kaitlin Schmidt grew up in Olympia. She recently graduated from Whitworth University and now lives in Spokane. She is currently a pastoral intern at Manito

Presbyterian Church and is grateful for her literary influence when interpreting the bible, the narratives of her community, and the narratives of her own life. She moonlights as a poet.

Nothing **Michael Schmidt** says is true. He was born in Seattle and is an MFA candidate in poetry writing at Eastern Washington University, where he also teaches English 101. He is alive to varying degrees. He exists in various places. Maple leaves are among his favorite things. He loves it when people tell him riddles. He loves meeting people. Water. One of Michael's favorite movie scenes is the one in *Magnolia* where all the frogs start falling from the sky. Michael is now an object.

Kathryn Smith's poems have appeared or are forthcoming in *Rock & Sling*, *Third Coast*, *The Cresset*, *Floating Bridge Review* and *RiverLit*. Her work has been published in the collections *Spokane Shorties* and *Lilac City Fairy Tales*, and she blogs for *Rock & Sling*. She received her MFA in poetry from Eastern Washington University. Born and raised on the Olympic Peninsula, she now lives in Spokane.

Christopher Stuck is a graduate student and teaching assistant in English at the University of South Carolina. He spent three years in Spokane while attending Eastern Washington University and embedded himself in the Spokane poetry scene. Many Spokanites may remember Christopher as the unofficial scorekeeper for Spokane Poetry Slam in its first year or for his prodigious red beard.

David Tagnani arrived from Pennsylvania in 2005 in order to pursue an MA in English at EWU, and he has been a Spokanite ever since. Currently, he is a PhD student at Washington State University, where he studies American Literature, mysticism, nature writing, and ecocriticism. He's also the Book Review Editor for the *Journal of Ecocriticism*. His poetry has appeared in *Camas*, *Written River*, *Kudzu Review*, and *Wilderness House Literary Review*.

John Allen Taylor was an urban farmer and poem-writer in Spokane, where he socialized feral kittens, made candles, and collected restaurantware from the early 1930s. After receiving a fellowship from Emerson College in Boston to attend their MFA in Creative Writing, he is in the process of uprooting, moving, and transplanting himself on the other coast. His hobbies will undoubtedly continue in an eastern fashion. He is the fiction editor for *Rock & Sling*, and he loves lentils. Even in real life he occasionally refers to himself in the third person; no one likes this.

Virginia Thomas is a senior in EWU's Creative Writing program. She was born and raised in Wyoming and moved to Spokane in 2013, where she now resides with her husband and their cat. Her love of poetry and literature come from her parents, who are both published writers. Her poems have been published in Northwest College's *Visualize Verbalize* and Eastern Washington's *Northwest Boulevard*.

Nance Van Winckel teaches in the low-residency MFA in Writing Program at Vermont College of Fine Arts. She is the author of five books of poetry and three collections of short stories. Her numerous awards include two National Endowment for the Arts Poetry Fellowships, a Pushcart Prize, two Washington State Artist Trust Awards, and *Poetry* magazine's Friends of Literature Awards. *After a Spell* won the Washington State Governor's Award for Poetry.

A former National Book Award finalist and winner of the Edgar Allan Poe Award, **Jess Walter** is the author of six novels, one book of short stories and one non-fiction book. His work has been translated into 30 languages, and his essays, short fiction, criticism and journalism have been widely published in *Best American Short Stories, Best American Nonrequired Reading, Harper's, Esquire, McSweeney's, Byliner, Playboy, ESPN the Magazine, Details,* and many others.

Ellen Welcker is the author of *The Botanical Garden* (winner of the 2009 Astrophil Poetry Prize, judged by Eleni Sikelianos), and the chapbooks *Mouth That Tastes of Gasoline* and *The Urban Lightwing Professionals.* She runs SpoPo, a living room reading series, coordinates The Bagley Wright Lecture Series on Poetry, and works as a Responder at EWU's Writers' Center. She is eager to thank Nate Pritts and *H_NGM_N* for first publishing the poems reprinted here.

John Whalen is the author of *Caliban,* and the chapbooks *In Honor of the Spigot* and *Above the Pear Trees.* His work has appeared in *Epoch, The Gettysburg Review, VQR,* and *CutBank.* While working in the printing and technology fields, he has also taught writing to students in elementary school, high school, and college, as well as to senior citizens in a psychiatric center. "Space Travel" was originally published in *YAWP* and also appeared in *Caliban.* "New Caledonia" first appeared in *Gettysburg Review,* and "Whatever Newly Complicates Us" was published in *CutBank*

Caitlin Wheeler is your standard mid-twenties MFA student, with long unkempt hair of a nondescript color, hobbies in watercolor and window-gazing, and a habit of canceling social plans. She studies fiction at the Inland Northwest Center for Writers, where she is the managing editor of Willow Springs Editions.

Joe Wilkins is the author of a memoir, *The Mountain and the Fathers: Growing up on the Big Dry,* winner of the 2014 GLCA New Writers Award and a finalist for the 2013 Orion Book Award, and two collections of poems. His work has appeared in *The Georgia Review, The Southern Review, Harvard Review, Ecotone, The Sun, Orion,* and *Slate,* among other magazines and literary journals. A Pushcart Prize winner and National Magazine Award finalist, he lives with his wife, son, and daughter in western Oregon, where he teaches writing at Linfield College. "Daybreak, Spokane, September 2001" originally published in *Killing the Murnion Dogs* (Black Lawrence Press 2011). "William T. Phillips" first appeared in *Notes from the Journey Westward* (White Pine Press 2012).

Tana Young holds a BA in English, writing & literature, art history minor, an MFA in creative writing, poetry emphasis, creative nonfiction minor. She taught English in Southeast Asia. Upon return, she began an MA program in Comp/Rhet. Her concentration is creative writing pedagogy.

Maya Jewell Zeller was born and raised in various coastal landscapes, but has now lived in Spokane longer than she has lived anywhere else. As a result she's taken to saying that her relationship to our city is like a (successful) arranged marriage: at first you may be skeptical, but in the long run you fall in love and can't imagine yourself with anyone else. Maya's book, *Rust Fish*, is available from Lost Horse Press. "Monroe Street: Route 24" first appeared in *New South*.